Martin Luther King

THE LIFE OF REVEREND DR MARTIN LUTHER KING JR

RICHARD S. REDDIE

LION

Copyright © 2011
This edition copyright © 2011 Lion Hudson

The author asserts the moral right
to be identified as the author of this work

A Lion Book
an imprint of
Lion Hudson plc
Wilkinson House, Jordan Hill Road,
Oxford OX2 8DR, England
www.lionhudson.com
ISBN 978 0 7459 5282 6

Distributed by:
UK: Marston Book Services, PO Box 269, Abingdon, Oxon, OX14 4YN
USA: Trafalgar Square Publishing, 814 N. Franklin Street, Chicago, IL 60610
USA Christian Market: Kregel Publications, PO Box 2607, Grand Rapids, Michigan 49501

First edition 2011
10 9 8 7 6 5 4 3 2 1 0

A catalogue record for this book is available
from the British Library

Typeset in 10/14 Photina MT
Printed and bound in China

Contents

	Introduction	6
CHAPTER 1	In the Beginning	15
CHAPTER 2	Dreaming Alive	26
CHAPTER 3	Changing Times	42
CHAPTER 4	The Times They are a-Changing	60
CHAPTER 5	I Have a Dream	85
CHAPTER 6	Eyes on the Prize	114
CHAPTER 7	Keep on Keeping on	138
CHAPTER 8	I May Not Get There with You	158
CHAPTER 9	Dreams to Remember	177
	Endnotes	184
	Bibliography	187
	Index	189
	Acknowledgments	192

INTRODUCTION

Above the Great West Door of the world famous Westminster Abbey in London stands a marble statue of Martin Luther King. Dr King is flanked by nine other twentieth-century Christian "martyrs" who lost their lives to religious, racial, and political intolerance. King is arguably the most famous of these ten marble effigies, which include Archbishop Oscar Romero and the less well known Chinese evangelist Wang Zhiming.

There is something curious and a tad jarring about seeing King's black visage represented in the shiny white stone. The incongruity of King's

The statue of the Reverend Dr Martin Luther King Jr stands between Oscar Romero (right) and the Grand Duchess Elizabeth of Russia (left) outside Westminster Abbey.

beautiful African features – full lips and broad nose – veiled in a pallid countenance gives his statue a surreal aspect. Yet this visual dissonance is very much a metaphor for the "whitewashing" of King's ideas and image since his assassination.

Over forty years after his assassination. King remains a colossus who is admired around the globe. His name has become synonymous with any struggle against injustice; he has ethical currency – many people cite King as the source of inspiration for their efforts to change a situation. In the USA both the political "left" and "right" use his words to justify a range of political decisions. King is beloved in Africa – he attended Ghana's independence celebrations in 1957, and saw real synergy between the struggles of Africans and African Americans to obtain real freedom.

He is admired in India, where he is likened to Mahatma Gandhi. The Dalits of that country see him as an inspiration in their fight for their rights. King famously visited the UK on his way to collect his Nobel Peace Prize in Oslo in December 1964, and his stay inspired the emergence of race equality organizations. And the inexorable rise of Black History Month, which is marked in October and February in the UK and USA respectively, is still a mainstay for lessons about King. In most societies that grapple with racism there are invariably calls for leaders in the vein of King who can be an advocate for minorities facing discrimination.

The advent of the first African-American president in the USA, King's homeland, has caused many to reassess his legacy, especially in the light of his legendary 1963 "I Have a Dream" speech, with its themes of brotherly love and peace. And it is this aspect of King which most people are familiar with – the colour-blind advocate of non-violence, the apostle of cheek-turning, who fused the best of Christ's and Gandhi's teachings to bring about change.

Ghana, West Africa,
where Martin Luther
King visited in
March 1957.

When I was a young man growing up in Bradford, West Yorkshire, King was second only to Jesus within our Christian household. He was educated, articulate and, most of all, moderate. The books I read about him were little more than hagiographies which presented a Christ-like figure who called on black people to love their white counterparts, irrespective of whether they were violent or hateful. This chimed with the Christian teachings I received on agape and sacrificial love. In the case of King, it asked black people to suffer to redeem a society that had excluded them. King was deemed the acceptable face of the civil rights struggle, one with whom white people felt comfortable, and one whose virtues they were keen to extol. This was in direct contrast to someone like Malcolm X, who had little time for non-violence or cheek-turning.

By the time I arrived at university, there was a resurgence of the black consciousness movement on both sides of the Atlantic, with an interest in all things African. This coincided with Spike Lee's cinematic release *Malcolm X*, a box office success which made the world more aware of the life of the black

Malcolm X, the African–American Muslim minister and human rights activist, speaks at a press conference. Malcolm X was a harsh detractor of white America for its perennial racism against African Americans. And for most of his public life he remained a critic of Martin Luther King.

Modern-day downtown Atlanta, Georgia, the city of Martin Luther King's birth.

Muslim activist. Unlike King, Malcolm X seemed to speak with unabashed pride about "blackness", and appeared to possess an analysis of the black condition that was relevant, credible, and timeless.

Malcolm X seduced me, as he did many of my peers. King's message and method became open to serious critique. In comparison to Malcolm X, King seemed a "meek and mild" figure who had little to say about the black condition in Britain, or elsewhere. His name appeared the embodiment of accommodation, and this disdain became all the more acute when those considered reactionaries peppered their speeches with his words. What made matters worse was the growing "King industry", which pumped out a range of materials presenting a sanctified image of a man who was all things to all people – only those who idolized Genghis Khan would have had a problem with him.

Yet, for a whole generation of young black people, this crossover appeal was regarded as a double-cross. We wanted an icon that was unapologetically black, whose words and ideas still spoke powerfully for a community that was considered the last, the least, and at times lost. King did not appear to do this, and as a result the initials "MLK" equated to "Meek Lightweight King", a man of acquiescence. And the Reverend Ralph Abernathy's controversial tome, *The Walls Come Tumbling Down*, which exposed King's many sexual indiscretions, only increased the cynicism toward him. When juxtaposed with Malcolm X, he appeared unable to match his Muslim counterpart's principles and philosophy.

My views on King changed radically after a visit to Atlanta, Georgia, in the mid 1990s. This trip gave me an opportunity to get behind the façade of the powerful image-making industry, to discover the real King. And it is this man that I seek to portray in this biography; a man who was always more of

a radical than a conservative, in both his social attitudes and politics. King's initial nuanced opinions on race, politics, war, economics, and American society were typical of his cautious radicalism. At the time of his death, the former *Time* magazine "Man of the Year" was virtually persona non grata among the political classes, and the purveyor of unpalatable truths for many erstwhile white American liberals.

It is my contention that the King myth was cemented by the "I Have a Dream" speech, with its utopian/heaven-like references to "all God's children" living together in harmony. Such has been the iconic impact of King delivering these evocative words from the podium at the Lincoln Memorial that they have come to define the man and his work. The events of that historic day are unhelpful for any serious assessment of King. That well-crafted and superbly delivered speech cast him as a "dreamer" and left him open to accusations that he ought to wake up to the nightmare facing African Americans. And it was this that led to the indictment that he was a colour-blind campaigner who cared more about putting white people at ease than dealing with the problems affecting African Americans. While it is true that King was no Malcolm X in his attitude to race issues, his complex but unambiguous approach held in tension a desire to create real racial harmony and integration in America with the necessity to affirm African-American self-worth and promote black agency.

King was also courageous and heroic. Unlike Malcolm X, who found himself in prison for larceny, King was incarcerated well over a dozen times for his stance on black rights and freedom. Moreover, he was prepared to use any means necessary, apart from violence, to effect change. He marched, petitioned, lobbied, lectured, preached and was arrested in the name of freedom. (He appeared to like his food too much to fast as his idol, Gandhi, did.) King was willing to face down detractors, both black and white, in order to explain his views. During the whole Black Power furore in 1966, he met with radicals to discuss his views on Black Power and black consciousness.

Thankfully, people are no longer asked to choose between the ideologies of King and Malcolm X for answers to the black condition. Both are two sides of the same coin, and there is clear evidence that they were heading in a similar leftward political direction at the time of their respective assassinations. Both were critical of unfettered capitalism, which they blamed for inequality and exploitation. King's critique of free enterprise was bound up in his censure of war, racism, and poverty. At this point in his life he was a radical or revolutionary, often to be found debating the Vietnam War with colourful characters linked to the counterculture. King's Poor People's Campaign planned to dramatize economic inequalities in Washington DC. King would not live to see his last audacious campaign, and while a single bullet would end his life, his legacy lives on today.

Barack Hussein Obama takes the oath as the USA's 44th president. With him is his wife, Michelle, and his daughters Malia and Sasha.

For some, the election of the first African-American president is the fulfilment of King's dream, in which a person is judged by the content of their character rather than their skin colour. Whether this is an accurate barometer by which to assess King's dream is open to debate; what is beyond doubt is that without King there would be no President Obama.

Most early accounts of King's life were trite and anodyne. Thankfully, critical scholarship, greater access to formerly secret FBI files, and Ralph Abernathy's autobiography have resulted in more rigorous, earthy depictions of King. In our highly critical, ultra judgmental age, those who are motivated more by prurience than scholarship have delved into every facet of King's (personal) life, leading some to question the measure of the man. Yet despite all this, King remains a hero and inspirational figure. His foibles and indiscretions appear to have humanized him, made his virtues attainable, and ideas accessible.

This book aims to offer a lively, highly informative yet thought-provoking reappraisal of a man whom many people "think they know". I am keen for readers to recognize there was more to King than "I Have a Dream", as he was a clever, complex, and sometimes conflicted man whom it has been hard to categorize. His theology, philosophy, and political opinions are profound and subtle. Above all, he was a man who lived and died trying "to love and serve humanity", and this book will reveal the struggles, pains, controversies, and triumphs connected to this.

Chapter 1
IN THE BEGINNING

The birth of a chubby black baby on 15 January 1929 was a singular moment of joy for Michael King Sr. Like all African-American preachers, he was pleased that God had given him a boy child who could continue the family name, and as such he gave his newborn his own name, Michael. The man the world would know as Reverend Dr Martin Luther King Jr would later describe his father as "strong in will as he is in his body", a trait that posed clear perils for African Americans during that era.

MICHAEL KING SENIOR

At the time of Michael King Sr's birth, the Southern states of the USA, with their sanctioning of segregation and rampant racism, proved a dangerous place for those of a darker hue. Georgia, where he was born, was a bastion of racism, and as a child he experienced discrimination in terms of insults and violence in his native Stockbridge. However, it was domestic violence that drove a fourteen-year-old King Sr from the family household. After grappling with his drunken father to defend his mother from a beating, the youth was sent to the thriving city of Atlanta to avoid patricide. Arriving in the city in 1918 with just the shirt on his back, the ambitious young man sought to better himself in a metropolis known for African-American businesses, especially the Sweet Auburn Historic District, a one-mile corridor that served as the downtown locale for Atlanta's black community. By sheer force of will, King Sr embarked on a series of measures to shake off his sharecropper's upbringing and become a "somebody". He enrolled in high school at a time when most students were leaving, and continued his studies into adulthood until he was a college graduate.

Martin Luther King Sr,
preaches his last sermon at
Ebenezer Baptist Church in
1975. King Sr had led the
church since 1931.

Like many African Americans looking for a social and spiritual lift,
King Sr turned to the church and began preaching, a profession which
proved useful when he began courting Alberta Williams, a plain, bashful
twenty-year-old who played the organ at Ebenezer Baptist Church, which
her father, A. D. Williams, pastored. Like King Sr, Reverend Williams
had fled his small-town, sharecropping background to make a new life
in Atlanta, and he saw something of himself in the suitor of his only
daughter. King Sr would eventually become a lodger in the Williamses'

house, where he continued his six-year courtship of Alberta. The couple would marry in November 1926, and begin a family the following year with the birth of a daughter, Willie Christine, in September 1927. At the time of his first son's birth, Michael King was still a student who combined his studies at the prestigious Morehouse College with the extra-curricular duties of an itinerant preacher. A third (and last) child, Alfred Daniel, or A. D., was born to the King family in 1930.

Such familial bliss was jolted by the death of the venerable A. D. Williams from a heart attack the following year, leaving a now graduated King Sr with the unenviable task of taking over his father-in-law's pulpit. The promotion of King to head of Ebenezer would later result in the moniker "Daddy" – a term of respect which denoted a potent patriarch. In Daddy King's situation it symbolized his growing authority within Atlanta's black community. One of his first duties as Ebenezer's head pastor involved boosting the coffers, since his church, like most finance-dependent concerns, was struggling during the Great Depression. Indeed, prior to Reverend Williams's death, cash-strapped congregants were often substituting food rather than finance for their offerings.

RACIAL SEGREGATION

It is debatable whether real austerity visited the King household during these straitened times, since Ebenezer's devoted congregants would have preferred to go in want than see their beloved pastor and his family endure hardship. The church and local community held Daddy King in high esteem, and he was given the respect afforded by his position. According to

King Jr "the first twenty-five years of my life were comfortable years", with Daddy King and Alberta doing their best to protect their son from the worst excesses of racial segregation in employment, commerce and public transport, and acts of violence perpetrated by the Ku Klux Klan and other vigilante groups.

Despite his parents' best efforts, King Jr, or "Mike", still experienced race-related indignities. On one occasion he shared his father's humiliation of being asked to take a back seat in a shoe store. When told he would not be served if he did not take a rear seat, a furious Daddy King retorted, "We'll either buy shoes sitting here or we won't buy any shoes at all," and he seized his son and fled the store. Daddy King's pride in his achievements left him unbowed to the crude racism of the South, and determined that his progeny would not face the same indignities. It was this steely minded attitude that enabled him to turn around Ebenezer's fortunes both financially and numerically, enabling congregants to finance his fact-finding journey to Europe and the Middle East in 1934. (This was virtually unheard of for a black Baptist minister at that time.) A part of this trip included a stay in Berlin, and it was in the German capital, home to St Mary's Church, or Marienkirche, famed for its statue of the Protestant reformer Martin Luther, that Daddy King took the momentous decision to change his Christian name from Michael to Martin.

On his subsequent return to the USA, the rechristened Martin King Sr similarly changed his five-year-old son's name, and thus changed history. Despite his new Christian name, King Sr was still known to most as Daddy King, a preacher who combined his pulpit duties with those of defending the rights of local African Americans, and his son would suggest he "always

A painting of Martin Luther (1483–1546), the German priest and theologian who initiated the Protestant Reformation.

[had] quite an interest in civil rights". Daddy King became the president of the local chapter of the National Association for the Advancement of Coloured People (NAACP) in Atlanta, leading the fight to equalize salaries and eliminate segregation in lifts and courthouses. One academic has argued that "decades prior to the Montgomery bus boycott, [Daddy] King's activism [meant he] refused to commute on a segregated bus system".[1] Daddy King's foray into civil rights led him on to a historic path trod by numerous individuals and organizations working for the betterment of African Americans.

THE STRUGGLE FOR "BLACK RIGHTS"

The struggle for "black rights" in the USA began during the long and cruel period of enslavement where Africans were held in perpetual bondage and considered as chattels. History reveals that almost 240 years passed until the Thirteenth Amendment to the US Constitution formally ended African enslavement in 1865. Yet it is still remiss in exploring the fundamental role played by African Americans who "resisted . . enslavement and non-citizenship ... or challenged emerging patterns of racial segregation...".[2] Pivotal to this struggle was the role of faith, since "much of what has transpired in the [USA] with respect to civil rights and social betterment has been envisioned and orchestrated by black churches, their pastors and members".[3] Enslaved Africans fused aspects of their traditional religions alongside Christianity to arrive at a belief system which challenged the racist, slave-dominated status quo. Heroic figures such as Philadelphia-born Richard Allen who, after purchasing his freedom in 1777, established his own Wesleyan-derived church, which "provided the organizational structure for black abolitionism, and inspired free blacks in other parts of the north to establish their own churches".[4] Equally, the infamous Nat Turner, who led a mass slave revolt in his native Virginia in 1831, was a Baptist minister "who believed himself to have a special purpose, or calling, from God that obligated him to work towards the freeing of enslaved blacks".[5] Likewise, the legendary abolitionist and statesman Frederick Douglass was a man of faith who believed he was in the tradition of "slave rebels like Gabriel [Prosser], Denmark Vesey and Nat Turner...".[6]

Although the Republican president Abraham Lincoln, spearheaded an anti-slavery-based civil war, there is evidence that he preferred to bar slavery from the territories rather than abolish the system in his efforts to keep the Union together and stave off conflict. His Emancipation Proclamation, which came into effect in January 1863, provided an authorized structure for the liberation of practically all enslaved African Americans (almost 4 million at that point). Lincoln also mused over giving African Americans the vote as part of the Reconstruction era, during which the economies and social structures of the USA, especially in the South, were restructured. Lincoln never lived to see the actual freedom of enslaved African Americans, as he was shot in April 1865. While the end of the Civil War and the onset of emancipation engendered relatively few improvements for most African Americans, many white Southerners interpreted the Reconstruction as a

Abraham Lincoln, the USA's 16th president.

ruse to promote black rule and eventual domination. Some disseminated wild accounts of black misrule in various Reconstruction states, leading to the emergence of vigilante groups such as the Ku Klux Klan, that were determined to put the "Negro" back in his place through acts of intimidation and violence.

Frederick Douglass emerged from the Civil War as the African American leader to whom the white establishment turned as the representative of his "race". He was arguably the first recognized national leader in an almost linear, undiminished line that led right up to Martin Luther King Jr nearly a century later. Douglass's efforts tended to focus on the plight of the newly emancipated African Americans who were forced to eke out an existence as sharecroppers – Southern farmers who leased land, accommodation, equipment, and credit from former planters and store holders respectively, in return for a portion of their crops. Such a loaded arrangement led to a perpetual indebtedness that tied these former enslaved people to the land much like debt bondage.

By 1875, the Republican-supporting Douglass became an ardent advocate of the Civil Rights Act passed to thwart prejudice in the South

A portrait of Frederick Douglass.

and champion voting rights and citizenship. He was criticized by African Americans as an "Uncle Tom" who was "handpicked by the white power structure...".[7] Similarly, his successor, Booker T. Washington, a former enslaved African, "owed his elevation as much to ... influential patrons ... as to his own remarkable abilities".[8] Washington assumed the mantle of leadership after Douglass's death in 1895. He implored African Americans to take their place in the world of commerce and industry, especially in the South, and appealed to white Southerners to give their black counterparts a chance, since they had always proved dependable and diligent. In his insightful autobiography, *Up From Slavery*, he charted his rise from a plantation in Franklin County, Virginia, to becoming the first African American to dine at the White House with President Theodore Roosevelt in 1901. The President was roundly criticized for this, with one senator, Benjamin Tillman, arguing that "the action of President Roosevelt in entertaining that [Negro] will necessitate our killing of a thousand [Negroes] in the South before they will learn their place again". Washington also faced criticism from African Americans such as W. E. B. Du Bois, who had once been an admirer, but who now denounced him as an "Uncle Tom" figure more interested in encouraging African Americans to undertake vocational professions such as farming techniques (men) and home economics (women), than directly tackling segregation and black political disenfranchisement. Others attacked Washington's "shrewd appetite for personal power and ... acceptance of indefinite racial subjection".[9]

In contrast to his predecessors, William Edward Burghardt (W. E. B.) Du Bois was born a free man in the Northern state of Massachusetts in

1868, and raised in the largely all-white community of Great Barrington. A gifted intellectual, Du Bois became the first African American to obtain a PhD from Harvard University in 1895 and took up teaching roles at Wilberforce University and the University of Pennsylvania. Like Washington, Du Bois believed that education was key to improving the lot of African Americans, but he believed that real economic advancement would be retarded by a lack of political engagement. His reputation as a leading thinker was cemented by the publication of his seminal work *The Souls of Black Folk*, in which he elaborated on his ideas such as the "double consciousness" of African Americans, in which there is an inherent tension in being a "Negro" and an American in the USA. His political activism was characterized by his role in the establishment of the NAACP in 1909, a multi-ethnic organization committed to "the political, educational, social, and economic equality of rights of all persons, and to eliminate racial hatred and racial discrimination". By the time of Martin Luther King Jr's birth, Du Bois's leadership had been challenged by more radical figures such as the Jamaican-born Marcus Mosiah Garvey, head of the United Negro Improvement Association (UNIA). For all his progressive ideas, Du Bois was still seen by some as an establishment lackey, and the black-conscious Garvey derided him as "the white-man's Negro who had never done anything yet to benefit Negroes".[10]

By the time Daddy King ascended to Ebenezer's pulpit, there was no shortage of African-American leaders, many of whom represented (faith) groups with political agendas. Chief among them was W. D. Fard's Nation of Islam, Eugene Kinckle Jones's National Urban League, Father Divine's International Peace Missions Movement, Reverends Adam Clayton Powell

*Daddy King's church,
like many in the South
at that time, was caught
up in America's fixation
with "race", especially
skin colour.*

Sr and Jr of the Abyssinian Baptist Church, the very light-skinned Walter Francis White of the NAACP (who often passed himself off as a white man), and the socialist-leaning A. Philip Randolph, president of the Brotherhood of Sleeping Car Porters (BSCP), a trade union supporting the many African-American staff working on the Pullman rail line. All these figures offered a variety of succour and salvation to African Americans during the Great Depression.

These organizations were also a response to the racism that impacted practically every aspect of African-American life and forced them to develop an alternative existence which often functioned alongside mainstream US society. In cities such as Atlanta, black people had their doctors, dentists, morticians, hair salons, barbers, grocery and general stores, nightspots, recreational facilities, and places of worship. The proprietors of these establishments, such as Daddy King, became men and women of some standing within the black community, who joined their professional activities with those as spokespeople for the black community.

Interestingly, Daddy King's church, like many in the South at that time, was caught up in America's fixation with "race", especially skin colour. During slavery, those Africans of a lighter hue (often the progeny of white slave masters and enslaved Africans) regarded themselves as superior to their darker skinned counterparts because "white blood" coursed their veins. This fixation with colour led to a "pigmentocracy" typified by those with lighter complexions invariably occupying more professional occupations within African-American society, making a false yet compelling juxtaposition between intelligence, aesthetical beauty, and sophistication. This concept also pervaded the black church, and it was not unknown for well-to-do congregations to apply the "comb test", which meant that any African American whose tresses were too "coarse" to pass through the comb's teeth was denied access or membership. Others were subjected to the "brown paper bag" test, where those whose complexions were darker than the coffee-coloured bag were denied entrance. Consequently, the African-American struggle for rights and equality not only involved a frontal struggle against white prejudice, but also a subtler fight to address "colourism".

Daddy King's involvement in the "freedom" movement was wholly consistent with that of a churchman and would-be community leader. However, it would be wrong to describe him as an earlier version of his son, since there was no theological analysis or defined strategy to his opposition to segregation. He invariably fought discrmination on an ad hoc basis – when it impacted him or those close to him. Yet he proved to be a defining influence on his son's understanding of segregation and the need to tackle the racism that saturated the South.

Chapter 2
DREAMING ALIVE

By his own admission, Martin or "M.L." enjoyed a home life that was as comfortable as it was stable, with his mother, Alberta, showering her eldest boy with much affection. According to many sources, the boy was a good scholar who learned quickly but lacked application, much to the consternation of his parents. For the authoritarian Daddy King, his son's "thoughtful inactivity" could be remedied by copious forms of corporal punishment. This caused him to clash with his wife who, although a stickler for good behaviour, had more liberal views on child chastisement. M.L.'s parents displayed more solidarity on how Christianity should inform his attitude to white racism in segregation-ridden Atlanta. The Kings gave M.L. a painful dinner table talk about racial etiquette in the South after he suffered the dual ignominy of a racial rebuff from the parents of a supposed white chum, and abuse from a white shopper.

His parents' dinner table homily would frame a conundrum that would test his spiritual and philosophical ideas for the rest of his life; namely, how as a Christian he could truly love those who were responsible for the racism that impacted every aspect of black life in the South. The situation was further compounded by the reality that many of these men and women described themselves as Christians. In numerous sermons and talks, M. L. would explore this vexatious matter, often struggling to hold in tension the theological chestnut of "loving the sinner but hating the sin". This apparent paradox was wrapped up in the wider theological poser of how a sovereign God could allow the perennial suffering of those African Americans who worshipped him.

As a boy, M. L. faced a daily form of racism when he took the segregated bus across town to the Atlanta University Laboratory School. The Lab School, as it was known, had been "created as an experiment to prove that high quality teachers could turn out black graduates every bit as skilled as white ones".[1] The school did its job, since on its closure due to the US war effort, M. L. was sufficiently advanced to enter Booker T. Washington High School as a thirteen-year-old. However, it was a still-traumatized M. L. who enrolled at Booker T. in 1942, having spent a year grieving for his beloved maternal grandmother, Jennie Williams. In M. L.'s youthful mind, his grandmother's sudden death was connected to a minor personal indiscretion, and the guilt-ridden boy attempted suicide by jumping from the second floor of his Atlanta home. A crippling sense of guilt over personal indiscretions would plague M. L. for the rest of his life.

FLOURISHING ACADEMICALLY

While Jennie Williams's death shook him up, it enabled M. L.'s father to fulfil a yearning to move to a larger house several blocks away – Alberta insisted that they keep the family home, which was rented out for additional income. Despite having to endure long segregated bus rides to the all-black Booker T. Washington High School, M. L. continued to flourish academically, adding discipline to his precocity. By his early teens, his education, coupled with his critical thinking, caused him to abhor the emotionally driven, experiential form of Christianity associated with black Baptist churches. He also began to question the central tenets of Christianity, such as the bodily resurrection of Jesus Christ. M. L. would subsequently build on such open-minded religious thinking when he attended the liberal Crozer Theological Seminary after graduating from Morehouse College.

By the age of fifteen, M. L. was suitably able to enter the prestigious Morehouse College as a freshman in September 1944. Under the leadership of the legendary president Dr Benjamin Mays, Morehouse had reduced its entrance age to compensate for a war-inspired cash shortfall. Dr Mays probably lowered academic standards as well, since by his own admission, M. L. "was still reading at only an eighth-grade level" when he enrolled at the college. And it was in the rarefied atmosphere of the historic university that he would embrace the pleasures of campus life, leaping headlong into dances, parties, and pool-playing. His college friends would later comment that his fixation with sartorial elegance was only matched by his predilection for the opposite sex. His particular clique of Morehouse Men went by the name of the "Wreckers" due to their penchant for "wrecking girls".[2] Even as a youth, M. L. oozed charm, but it was during his Morehouse years that he would hone both this and his linguistic dexterity to devastating effect.

M. L.'s Morehouse undergraduate days were distinguished by his interaction with the eminent Dr Mays, a gifted theologian and fellow Baptist whom he would later describe as "one of the great influences on his life".[3] When not listening to Dr Mays, he was studying Henry David Thoreau's 1849 "Essay on Civil Disobedience", which brought to his attention the theory of non-violence, and the "idea of refusing to cooperate with an evil system". In his penultimate undergraduate year, M. L. took the momentous decision to become a minister of religion. He opted for this career despite failing to find answers to the lingering spiritual questions that had emerged during his early teens. There is evidence that his studies at Morehouse only served to multiply these religious posers;

*Crozer proved to
be the making of
M. L., turning him
from a provincially
minded individual
to a rounded,
urbane intellectual.*

consequently, his resolution to enter the clergy was a rational one devoid of any Pauline-like revelation or heavy emotionalism. M. L. had often contemplated serving "God and humanity" in some capacity which, coming from his particular family background, would logically point toward the pulpit. For Daddy King, this news was as sweet as anything sung by Ebenezer's choir, and went some way toward redeeming his son's far from excellent academic record at Morehouse.

M. L. graduated from Morehouse College in 1948 with a sociology degree, and a promising future alongside his father in Ebenezer's pulpit beckoned. Daddy King's joy of having his eldest boy serve as his assistant was soon dented when M. L. confirmed that he intended to continue his studies at Crozer Theological Seminary in far-off Pennsylvania. Daddy King's academic education had ended after Morehouse, and he could not fathom why his son wanted to pursue further studies, especially ones at a liberal seminary that was known to cool the ardour of many an "on-fire" evangelical. Notwithstanding its theology, Crozer was a progressive institution where the sprinkling of black, mainly Baptist, seminarians mixed freely with their white counterparts on campus, often sharing dormitories, bedrooms, and beds. (Such utopian ideas did not sit well with all the white students, particularly the Southern ones, and this led to the inevitable racial tensions.)

THE MAKING OF THE MAN

Crozer proved to be the making of M. L., turning him from a provincially minded individual to a rounded, urbane intellectual. Unlike the all-black Morehouse, Crozer enabled M. L. to interact with white students, and this

Karl Heinrich Marx.

brought out a competitive streak in him. As a son of the South, M. L. had grown up against a backdrop of racial stereotypes that had their roots in American slavery, which presented African Americans as lazy, unclean, crude, stupid, and ill-disciplined. Mindful of this, he went overboard in presenting himself as everything contrary to these racial myths. Like his subsequent hero, the actor Sidney Poitier, M. L. was one of the few black faces in a thoroughly white space, and believed he had to "represent the race" and present "his people as positively as he could".[4] By his own admission, he was conscientious in every sense of the word, and totally committed to academic excellence.

Such diligence bore fruit, and the young student would often continue his studies well into the night, studying everything from the Greek philosophers to the Enlightenment. He discovered Karl Marx, spending the Christmas holidays of 1949 studying *Das Kapital* and *The Communist Manifesto*. Although he would publicly reject communism, arguing that it was "basically evil" because of its "metaphysical materialism, ethical relativism, and political totalitarianism", his thinking from that point on would be influenced by Marxism, taking him in an entirely new direction toward the end of his life. Daddy King had little time for his son's growing fascination with communism and critique of capitalism (or his developing theological ideas), which he linked to Western democracy and freedom. Under the tutelage of Robert Keighton, M. L. commenced a preaching ministry course which, among other subjects, taught the dynamics of "how to preach and assemble a sermon". For an aspiring preacher with a penchant for oratory, these classes gave his sermons a panache that would impress as much as confuse, and during his holidays at Ebenezer, many of his father's congregants. while marvelling at his eloquence, were forced to consult dictionaries after his sermons.

THE "SOCIAL GOSPEL"

In his second year at Crozer, a lecture by the inveterate pacifist A. J. Muste brought the topic of pacifism onto M. L.'s academic radar. For most Americans, who were four years out of the Second World War, pacifism was unAmerican – a sop to the machinations of bellicose regimes, especially during the Cold War. Though M. L. initially shared these views, his ideas would alter dramatically when he learned of the teachings of Mohandas K. Gandhi via a talk by the Howard University president Mordecai Johnson, who had just returned from India.

Crozer also enabled M. L. to synthesize the evangelicalism of his African-American Baptist heritage with the liberal theology espoused by the seminary. It exposed him to the "Social Gospel", a US Protestant movement dating back to the nineteenth century, which regarded the social problems caused by rapid industrialization and rampant capitalism a moral threat to church and society. By the turn of the twentieth century, the Social Gospel was a mainstay at many seminaries, including Crozer, which became a bastion for "Social Gospeller"

> *Any real fight against injustice would need to combine theological methods with political force.*

theologians and philosophers, whose teachings and ideas would greatly influence M. L. Chief among them was Walter Rauschenbusch, an American Baptist theologian of German ancestry whose seminal publications *Christianity and the Social Crisis* (1907) and *Theology for the Social Gospel* (1917) argued that the kingdom of God "is not a matter of getting individuals to heaven, but of transforming the life on earth into the harmony of heaven". Rauschenbusch argued that Jesus' teachings were as much, if not more, about social justice as personal transformation. In his first book, *Stride Toward Freedom*,[5] M. L. waxed lyrical about Rauschenbusch's firm belief in society's "chances of real advancement" and "humanity's potential for improvement on various levels", which chimed with his own beliefs on transformation and advancement.

NEO-ORTHODOXY

Another American of German ancestry, Reinhold Niebuhr, was to have an even greater impact on M. L.'s study and life. Alongside fellow theologian Paul Tillich, Niebuhr was a chief proponent of the "Neo-Orthodoxy" movement of the 1930s that was a response to the previous century's liberal theology doctrines. In his seminal book, *Moral Man and Immoral Society*, Niebuhr described his move from liberal theology to "Christian Realism" which critiqued the Social Gospel as "misplaced and naïve", as it failed to "measure adequately the power and persistence of man's self-concern".[6] Niebuhr's ideas highlighted the "complexity of human motives and the reality of sin on every level of man's existence". This "spoke directly to King's natural interest in Christian perspectives on the pervasiveness of racial discrimination and segregation". M. L. would read that Christian love, as great as it was, had its limitation because of sin; and therefore any real fight against injustice would need to combine theological methods with political force. One writer has argued that "Niebuhr's influence went to the heart of the public and private King and affected him more deeply than did any modern figure, including Gandhi...".[7]

Unlike at Morehouse, M.L. excelled academically at Crozer and "gained high marks from his professors, and the confidence of his fellow students who voted him class president".[8] As in his undergraduate days, he continued to shoot pool and play cards with friends, once again to the chagrin of his father, who considered such pastimes sinful and the preserve of lower class individuals. Daddy King also took a dim view of his beer drinking and cigarette smoking (M. L. would sometimes smoke a pipe for dramatic effect). M. L. also maintained his reputation as a ladies' man on campus with a number of romantic affiliations. One such relationship, which occurred in his third year, involved the daughter of the seminary's German cook, a winsome girl named Betty. This affiliation was scandalous at the time, not only because of the girl's seemingly low status, but also because she was white. In the cosseted, liberal environment of Crozer, such an interracial liaison raised eyebrows, but allowed the couple an opportunity to develop their relationship. M. L. became smitten and was adamant that Betty was wife material, much to the consternation of friends who knew that very few churches (black or white) would accept an African-American clergyman with a white spouse. The various pressures forced a reluctant M. L. to call an end to this relationship and he left Crozer with a broken heart, but the best academic grades in his class.

With his academic appetite thoroughly whetted, M. L. continued his studies at Boston University, arriving on campus in September 1951 in a new green sedan (a graduation gift from his parents) to pursue a doctorate in philosophy and theology. Under the tutelage of Edgar Brightman and Harold DeWolf, he came under the influence of their "personalist" theories, which rejected the notion that God was "an abstract being". M. L. would subsequently argue that God was not a "divine hermit hiding himself in a cosmic cave", but "possessed a personality, and [could] therefore have a relationship with human beings".[9] He would extrapolate that every person should be afforded dignity and respect because, unlike other created beings, men and women were fashioned for the unique purpose of replicating God's nature. Therefore, if individuals (from every ethnic group) are created in the image of God (*Imago Dei*) there could be no place in society for racism. M. L. would later contend that the Bible did not tolerate racism, as this saddened the heart of God, and that it was the duty of every individual to work to construct a "beloved community" on earth.

M. L. excelled at Boston; he was a well-read, critical thinking student open to new ideas and theories. His study of Hegel's system of dialecticism with its thesis, antithesis and synthesis stages of development would influence his decision-making and leadership of the Southern Christian Leadership Conference, much to the annoyance of some in that organization. However, his fixation with "personalism" and Hegel was not the only academic predisposition he developed at Boston University; subsequent research has shown he acquired the tendency to lift extracts from the works of others without the appropriate citation.[10] This form of plagiarism found its way into his doctoral thesis, "A comparison of the conception of God in the thinking of Paul Tillich and Henry Nelson Wieman", which included a crib from a former Crozer student, and other secondary sources. Equally, his academic papers failed to include quotation marks and footnotes to make clear his usage of others' material.

The jury is still out on whether M. L. intentionally committed one of the gravest academic transgressions, and his apologists have suggested his actions were more a result of sloppiness than malfeasance. Yet this habit of playing fast and loose with the works of others found its way into his books, speeches, and sermons, leading one writer to compare him to contemporary hip hop artistes who often "sample" and/or pass off the works of others as their own.[11] Likewise, the writers Lewis V. Bladwin and Richard Lischer have noted that M. L. came from a preachers' tradition that frequently refashioned and recycled the sermons of other clergymen.[12]

It was also during his tenure at Boston that M. L. was to meet and marry the woman who would transform his life, Coretta Scott. Prior to meeting her in January 1952, M. L. continued his "princely" antics around campus, using his dapper appearance, fancy green Chevrolet, and smooth talk to date fellow students Juanita Sellers and Mary Powell. And it was Powell who would introduce M. L. to Coretta, an Alabama native who was two years his senior. Powell gave M. L. Coretta's number and he wasted no time calling his latest pursuit, launching into a shameless line of flattery where he described himself as "Napoleon at Waterloo" and brought "to his knees". The flannel worked since she agreed to meet him for lunch the following day.

If classical male beauty is epitomized by the categories of "tall, dark and handsome" – M. L. was dark. Standing no more than five feet seven inches, he lacked the imposing stature of his future nemesis Malcolm X. Nor could he be described as an Adonis, not possessing the drop-dead sex appeal of the strikingly handsome Harry Belafonte, the African-American entertainer and future comrade in the civil rights struggle. His physical attributes, or the lack of them, were borne out by Coretta's comments,

The beautiful Coretta Scott King,
wife of Martin Luther King.

who, on their first meeting, described her future husband as, "This little
man who was so short ... [and who didn't] look like much." She was later
to enthuse about his capacity to "talk" and "radiate charm" – traits that
M. L. had in abundance. The couple's first tryst went well, with M. L.
allowing his gift of the gab to go into overdrive, conversing on everything
from food to philosophy and belief to beauty. The couple swapped family
histories and realized they were both middle children with an elder female
sibling and a younger male one. Equally, they had single-minded, bull-
headed fathers who were prepared to confront segregation in the interests
of personal freedom. M. L. appeared to have made up his mind on his first
date that he had met his future wife, as Coretta had the four things he liked,
namely "character, intelligence, personality and beauty".

COURTING CORETTA

The couple began to date throughout 1952, and their courtship included visits
to concerts, recitals, and plays. Coretta became a regular at M. L.'s apartment,
adding a woman's touch to the bachelor-like feel of his living space. M. L.
would speak about her to his parents, who became aware of the seriousness
with which he was taking this new relationship. The situation came to a head
in August 1952, when he took Coretta south to meet his family. Ensconced
in their fetching residence, she found the King clan reserved to the point of
aloofness, while the patriarchal Daddy King was positively unreceptive. King
Sr had become increasingly concerned over his son's growing affection for
Coretta and he feared that his eldest boy might choose this "country gal"
over one of the "maidens" he had lined up from Atlanta's better-connected

families. Unlike M. L., who was very much a child of privilege, Coretta was from humble, rural stock. Her father, Obadiah Scott, was an industrious farmer who supplemented his income by cutting hair at the family home in the evenings. His diligence, which resulted in his ownership of a sawmill and a truck, would provide financial stability for his family. However, unlike the Morehouse-educated Daddy King, both he and his wife, Bernice McMurray Scott, remained unschooled. This was undoubtedly the driving force behind their determination to see their children educated at the best schools, albeit ones that were racially segregated. Coretta passed through the schools system, graduating aged eighteen from Lincoln Normal School in 1945. She continued her education – in music – at the racially mixed Antioch College in Ohio, where her elder sister, Edythe, had become its first African-American scholar. Like many an aspiring African-American student from the South, she was keen to move away from segregation, and regarded education as a means of advancement. However, she faced prejudice when the college failed to support her request to teach in an all-white faculty at a public school. Furious at this decision, Coretta joined the local branch of the NAACP and took a greater interest in other progressive organizations committed to addressing segregation. This was in stark contrast to M. L., who took greater interest in Karl Marx and philosophy than race issues as a student.

Sharing her parents' educational ambitions, Coretta moved further north to Boston where, courtesy of a scholarship, she read music at the noted New England Conservatory. At this point she had designs on becoming a concert singer, and in between her studies she honed her modus operandi in choirs and choral groups. When not singing, she found time to go on that first eventful date with M. L. By the time Daddy King had begun registering

The smiling Kings: Martin Luther King and Coretta share a close moment.

his concerns about her, she had fallen for his son in a big way and was rapidly succumbing to his overtures of marriage.

By his own admission, Daddy King usually got his way in family related matters, and he made his opposition to any betrothal very clear. However, the usually deferential M. L. refused to bow to his father's demands, which resulted in unresolved tensions between them. M. L. found real support in Coretta, who although intimidated by the imposing Daddy King, was a woman of singular resolve and knew her own mind. This proved useful when Daddy King, somewhat concerned about his son's waning inclination to call home, travelled to Boston for a showdown. In response to his question about whether she was "serious about his son", Coretta mistakenly told the sombre-minded clergyman "No". This only vexed the patriarch, who rolled off the names of the women who were suitable marriage material for his son – much to the bewilderment of Coretta. M. L. was forced to confront his father about his wedding plans, laying down the ultimatum that Coretta "would be his wife regardless of what his father thought or said". According to Daddy King, his son confessed: "I know that you don't really approve, but this is something I have to do."

Daddy King would subsequently acquiesce to M. L.'s wishes and officiate over his marriage in June 1953 at Coretta's family home in Alabama. The newlyweds' first night of wedded bliss was spent in the less than salubrious surroundings of the first floor of a friend's funeral parlour. They later moved into the Kings' family home for the summer, with the now-styled Coretta Scott King obtaining a post at the black-owned Citizen's Trust Bank where Daddy King was a director. As well as a name change, she also switched her denominational affiliations from lifelong Methodist to newly baptized – at the hands of Daddy King – Ebenezer Baptist member, taking her place in the congregation while M. L. carried out his pastoral duties with his father. At the end of the summer, the couple travelled to Miami to join M. L.'s parents for the National Baptist Convention before returning to Boston for M. L. to finish his doctoral studies.

January 1954 saw M. L. at a career crossroads. With a wife to support he looked for a job which he could combine with his PhD dissertation on the theologians Tillich and Wieman. And as he approached the completion of his studies, he was unsure whether to pursue an academic career at a university, as befitting someone with a doctorate, or follow the more obvious option of the pulpit. The latter would have pleased Daddy King, who naturally expected his son to join him full-time at the burgeoning Ebenezer. The academic in M. L. was concerned that his learning would be wasted in black Baptist churches, which in his opinion valued emotionalism and verve over intellect and rationalism. The one issue over which there was no uncertainty was his desire to move out of Daddy King's shadow, which meant any return to the South had to be away from his native Atlanta.

M. L.'s intention of settling in the South placed early tensions on the Kings' eventful marriage. Unlike her husband, Coretta had less emotional attachments to Dixie, and had essentially fled its myriad restrictions to pursue

A young Martin Luther King preaches at Ebenezer Baptist Church.

studies and a potential career as a classical singer in the North. Although her chances of becoming an African-American soloist were decidedly limited, the North's relative latitude enabled her to take advantage of a range of cultural activities in keeping with her tastes. Life in the South held out few such desegregated cultural outlets for African Americans, and her existence would be reduced to that of a prominent clergyman's wife and homemaker. (Coretta's status within the Kings' marriage would always be a bone of contention, with the less than progressive M. L. insisting that his capable and ambitious wife look after their children rather than involve herself in activism.)[13]

In January 1954, M. L. was invited to deliver a trial sermon – a preaching job interview – at Dexter Avenue Baptist, an affluent, conservative African-American church in Montgomery, the state capital of Alabama. Dexter was the former tenure of the charismatic, controversial preacher Dr Vernon Johns, whose exploits at the church included halting the weddings over which he was officiating to advertise the wares he sold on a horse and cart, and concluding his hard-hitting sermons with a benediction that mentioned the watermelons or fish he was retailing after the service. After several years of such scandalizing, Dexter Avenue's snooty leadership finally called Dr Johns' bluff by asking him to resign.

Dexter's officious church leaders and its haughty congregation were suitably impressed with M. L.'s trial sermon, "The Three Dimensions of a Complete Life", and invited him to become its latest pastor, agreeing to make him the best paid clergyman in Montgomery. While Daddy King dismissed the role as a poison chalice, M. L. saw the post as an apposite challenge for a twenty-five-year-old college graduate who needed space and an opportunity to develop as his own man.

DREAMING ALIVE

Chapter 3
CHANGING TIMES

Accompanied by his less than enthusiastic wife, an excited M. L. took up his clerical duties at Dexter Avenue Baptist Church in September 1954. Although Daddy King had been firmly against his son taking up the post, he nonetheless made the 350-mile round trip to attend his installation, taking the bulk of his Ebenezer congregation with him for moral support. And while he may have been unhappy with his son's initial career choice, he would have been proud of his resolute approach to reforming Dexter's rigid structures, which involved loosening the authoritarian grip of the deacons who had occasioned Vernon Johns' downfall. M. L. insisted that his authority to lead came from God, and he implemented organizational changes such as inserting his people into strategic positions on committees. He also reorganized the offerings and established church clubs to ensure the Sunday collection reflected the finances of his well-heeled congregation.

In order to start as he meant to go on, M. L. awoke just after dawn to work on his PhD dissertation (he had insisted that Dexter meet the costs of his commuting to Boston University for tutorials), and his hectic daily work schedule included sermon preparation, speaking engagements, pastoral duties, and church administration, leaving whatever time remained for Coretta. Yet despite his assiduous labours, Dexter was never able to usurp the Reverend Ralph Abernathy's Montgomery First Baptist as the city's biggest black church. According to one writer, "Dexter Avenue ... was the place to go if one wished to experience the messages of Socrates, Aquinas, and Hegel in their contemporary relevance. For straightforward preaching, one went to Ralph's [Abernathy] Montgomery First Baptist. The atmosphere lent itself to shouts of 'amen', shrieks of joy, and general getting to the nitty

Dexter Avenue Baptist Church in Montgomery, Alabama. Dexter was Martin Luther King's first church, and the headquarters for the Montgomery bus boycott.

gritty of things"[1]. Although Ralph Abernathy could have been a potential rival, he was one of the first to welcome M. L. to town, the two having previously met at a Baptist convention.

Ralph David Abernathy was an Alabama native and a World War Two veteran who, after graduating from the state university, had made a circuitous route into the pulpit. Three years older than M. L., he shared the latter's physical stature, but none of his complexities, since he was, to quote one writer, "Mr Rough [to M. L.'s] Mr Smooth".[2] Abernathy would use his more earthy approach as a foil to his companion's loftier pretensions when he became M. L.'s "warm-up" man at speeches. On a deeper level, he became M. L.'s foremost confidant, the person who would arguably spend more time with M. L. than anyone else (including Coretta), during the latter part of his life.

Notwithstanding the demands of reorganizing his church, M. L. was still able to submit his PhD dissertation, for which he received a doctorate in the summer of 1955. Not content with stamping his authority on Dexter's

Left: The Dynamic Duo: a waving Martin Luther King stands beside his long-time friend and confidant Ralph Abernathy during a visit to London, England.

Below: Racial segregation permeated every aspect of life in the Southern United States, even the US army.

lay leadership, he also set out to impose himself on Montgomery's large black community, a population scarred by decades of searing segregation. At the time of his arrival, Montgomery was completely segregated, with its bars, restaurants, schools, buses, toilets, sports facilities, and lunch counters prohibiting the mixing of African Americans and white citizens. The city's 50,000 African Americans endured the lion's share of dilapidated housing, poor schools and menial jobs, and their entire existence appeared geared toward meeting the needs of the 70,000 white people as servants, butlers, chauffeurs, nannies, or general labourers.

Symptomatic of this disenfranchisement was the fact that only 2,000 African Americans were registered voters. When M. L. became aware of this figure he insisted that all Dexter members become registered voters and supporters of the NAACP. This was not to suggest that segregation had made the African-American community docile. The aforementioned Vernon Johns was a civil rights activist whose sermons and acts of civil disobedience challenged segregation. Likewise, Montgomery-born Edgar Daniel (E. D.) Nixon was a veteran activist and union leader who led the Pullman Porters Union (the Montgomery branch of the larger Brotherhood of Sleeping Car Porters Union), and also headed the local chapter of the NAACP.

Many simplistic accounts of the civil rights movement tend to reduce the role of women to that of Rosa Parks, yet long before the world had heard of Mrs Parks, women such as Jo Ann Robinson, who was president of the Women's Political Council and an academic at the celebrated Alabama State College, had opposed segregation on local buses. Robinson had her first major transport-related altercation in 1949 when she confronted the abuse of a white bus driver. By the early 1950s, she had joined forces with E. D. Nixon to oppose Montgomery's bus segregation; and in keeping with NAACP methods, they challenged racist seating practices in the law courts. The political stirrings occurring in Montgomery reflected activities elsewhere; the African-American community in Baton Rouge, Louisiana, began a transport boycott in June 1953 that would be reminiscent of its more famous successor in Montgomery a few years later. Under the headship of Reverend T. J. Jemison, a pastor and former NAACP leader, church leaders formed the United Defense League, which encouraged local people to stay away from buses. Although the campaign ended with a compromise, it was "the first mass, direct action campaign led by [black] church leaders".[3]

The killing of Emmett Till in August 1955 proved a pivotal moment in Southern race relations and civil rights. Till was a carefree fourteen-year-old African American who lived in Chicago, but was visiting relatives in Mississippi when he was killed by a group of white men. Till's "crime" was allegedly whistling at or talking to a young white woman as he left a local grocery store. When the authorities recovered his bloated corpse from the Tallahatchie River, it was so disfigured it could only be identified by a ring he wore. A month later, an all-white jury cleared the two white men charged with his murder, creating uproar among local African Americans, and greater interest in civil rights.

Prosecutors deliberate during the trial of the murdered teenager Emmett Till in September 1955.

The upsurge in Southern activism mirrored what was occurring nationally with the United States Supreme Court's historic decision on Brown v. Board of Education of Topeka, Kansas, judgment, which declared separate public schools for African American and white pupils unlawful, and the denial of equal educational chances for African Americans' illegal. The Supreme Court's judgment reversed the 1896 Plessy v. Ferguson decision, which under the doctrine of "separate but equal" preserved the constitutionality of segregation among the races in public accommodation such as schools. According to the writer Philip Jenkins the "Brown decision contributed to a spreading of the protest movement across the south, which found a symbol in 1955 when Rosa Parks of Montgomery, Alabama, refused to yield a bus seat to a white passenger".[4]

According to common lore, on Thursday 1 December 1955 Rosa Parks, a bespectacled forty-two-year-old seamstress, boarded a single-decker bus on Montgomery's Cleveland Avenue, heading home after a hard day's work and Christmas shopping. Parks, like all Montgomery's bus passengers, was used to a segregated system in which white passengers took a bus's front row seats, filling toward the back, while black customers took seats in the back rows, filling the bus toward the front, where in due course the two sections would meet.[5] If a white person boarded a full bus, those in the "black row" closest to the front had to get up and stand, so that a new row for white passengers could be created. (Black passengers would have to stand if the bus was full or if there were empty seats in the white section.) African-American passengers also endured the racist abuse of white drivers who "routinely ... referred to [them] as ni--ers and black apes".[6]

On that fateful day, a tired Rosa Parks refused to give her seat to a white man who boarded three stops later. The white bus driver, James F. Blake, who had ordered three African Americans from their seats, could not persuade Parks to do likewise, leading to her arrest. This spontaneous response to bus segregation supposedly started the modern civil rights movement in the USA. A closer examination of events reveals anything but spontaneity, since the bookish-looking Parks was a long-time activist (she was the volunteer secretary for the NAACP chapter in Montgomery) with "previous" for such protests. In 1943, she had experienced her first encounter with bus driver Blake over which entrance she had to use to board his bus. Her husband, Raymond Parks, was also an NAACP member, and his chapter of the organization had spent some time looking for a suitable case which it could use to challenge the city's segregated transport system.

Indeed, Parks was not the first African-American woman to be arrested for refusing to give up her seat; nine months earlier, fifteen-year-old student Claudette Colvin had been detained for refusing to relinquish her place to a white female passenger. However, the NAACP's E. D. Nixon, and lawyers Clifford Durr and Fred Gray, failed to take up Colvin's case as she was deemed an "unsuitable role model". The teenager, who allegedly cursed profoundly on being arrested, was from a humble background and found to be pregnant by a married man – factors which the legal team believed could detract from any legal challenge. By contrast, Rosa Parks was a married, middle-aged, educated, churchgoing woman whose calm, measured appearance belied her keen political nous. Additionally, she was a known quantity, who was cognizant of the consequences of civil disobedience in segregated Montgomery.

News of Parks' arrest soon hit the grapevine, mobilizing E. D. Nixon, Jo Ann Robinson, and a phalanx of clergy. Nixon went to the jail house to bail his NAACP colleague, and organized a meeting of mainly local clergy because the church "bridged the social classes and political factions and could provide meeting places and fundraising machinery".[7] In the meantime, the ever-active Robinson produced and distributed a flyer which called for a boycott of the city's buses the following Monday. Ironically, work pressures meant that Nixon could not attend the meeting he had called, and in his absence M. L. was appointed head of the Montgomery Improvement Agency, or MIA, which was tasked with taking forward the bus boycott. Had Nixon attended, history may have taken a different course.

THE BIRMINGHAM BUS BOYCOTT

Certainly M. L. did not actively seek a role that would place him at the forefront of a movement which would confront Montgomery's powerful, intransigent power structure. For one thing, he had just become a father

Martin Luther King Jr stands in front of a newly integrated bus in December 1956 after the year long boycott in Montgomery.

for the first time when Coretta gave birth to Yolanda Denise (or "Yoki") in November 1955, and he was keen to spend as much time with his new daughter as possible. Equally, he was aware that as the new kid in town, his leadership may have been resented by long-time Montgomery civil rights activists. However, his supporters regarded this as an asset; Rosa Parks was later to suggest: "The advantage of having Dr. King as president was that he was so new to Montgomery and to civil rights work that he hadn't been there long enough to make any strong friends or enemies."[8] After receiving Coretta's backing, M. L. agreed to become MIA's president, with E. D. Nixon taking on the role of treasurer. Both would oversee a bus boycott that would begin the following Monday.

An apprehensive M. L. rose early that Monday morning, not sure what to expect. As two-week-old Yoki slept on, he was surprised to hear Coretta shout, "Martin, Martin, come quickly!" And, pointing out of the window, she added, "It's empty," referring to the first bus of the morning which passed their house. Most African Americans in Montgomery took the buses to work, so it was a surprised but pleased M. L. who observed a bus bereft of black passengers. Both the second and third buses were in a similar state, and that first day nine out of ten African Americans stayed off Montgomery's buses.

That evening, M. L. spoke to a large crowd at Holt Street Baptist Church. With very little time to prepare for his talk, he was determined to ensure that their firm stance remained within a Christian context. By now the events of the day had become news, and with the TV cameras rolling and the flashbulbs going off in his face, M. L. took to the pulpit to deliver what he later described as "the most decisive speech of my life".

He spoke without notes, using his sonorous voice and command of the English language to set out a narrative that would define not only the bus boycott, but also the wider struggle for civil rights. Wiping the sweat off his boyish face he began, "We are here this evening for serious business. We are here in a general sense because first and foremost we are American citizens and we are determined to apply our citizenship to the fullness of its meaning." With an attentive, highly charged audience listening on he continued, "You know, my friends, there comes a time when people get tired of being trampled over by the iron feet of oppression ... There comes a time when people get tired of being pushed out of the glittering sunlight of life's July, and left standing amid the piercing chill of an alpine November." Punctuated by the audience's "Amens", he spoke about the indignities of Rosa Parks and myriads of African-American passengers who had been abused by Montgomery's bus drivers.

He continued: "I want it to be known that we're going to work with grim and bold determination to gain justice on the buses in this city. And we are not wrong ... If we are wrong, the Supreme Court of this nation is wrong. If we are wrong, the Constitution of the United States is wrong. If we are wrong, God Almighty is wrong." He implored his listeners that enough was enough, and that the time had come to bring about change. But he argued that only a unity underpinned by the Christian virtues of love and justice could bring about this much-needed transformation. He finished with the race-conscious statement, "There lived a race of people, a black people, fleecy locks and black complexion, a people who had the moral courage to stand up for their rights. And thereby they injected a new meaning into the veins of history and of civilization."

The assembly adopted the MIA's initial resolution, which was modest to say the least. Rather than calling for an immediate end to bus segregation, the organization demanded polite treatment for all bus passengers; a first-come, first-served seating policy, which saw African Americans seated at the back and whites at the front; and increased hiring of African Americans as bus drivers. M. L. knew the bus company stood to lose around $3,000 a day in revenue and that this would have a knock-on effect in lost taxes, and sales in department stores. He was also cognizant that the local White Citizens Council, which had been formed after the 1954 Brown v. Board of Education judgment to maintain segregation and white hegemony, would use the law and any other means to put the kibosh on black demands.

For the boycott to work, the MIA had to find an alternative means of ferrying passengers to and from their destinations. Initially, Montgomery's black-owned taxi companies were pressed into service, with drivers instructed to charge no more than the usual bus fare. When this mode of transport ran into legal problems, they came upon the idea of establishing a carpool, which saw those with vehicles used as would-be taxis. At its height around 3,000 cars were involved, while others used non-motorized modes of transport such as bicycles, mule and cart, or plain old Shanks's pony. There were even instances of white women driving their female domestic employees to work; some out of solidarity, others out of self-interest.

Montgomery's white population was initially wrong-footed by the boycott, as all previous acts of black militancy had been random, small, and invariably ended in glorious failure due to outward white pressure and internal black wrangling. Totally unused to such black-based activism on this scale, they apportioned it to outside (Northern) influences. For

Montgomery's white power structure, any victory would have been a slippery slope leading to the destruction of the city's social fabric, and so it swung into action, scouring through the legal annals to enact any by-law that would undermine the boycott. The city commissioner, Clyde Sellers, the mayor, William A. "Tacky" Gayle, and Commissioner Frank Parks joined the White Citizens Council and, as a result, black taxi firms were threatened with fines if they charged a passenger less than forty-five cents. Moreover, drivers involved in the carpools were told they could not charge passengers for rides, and that this usage of their vehicles violated the terms of their agreed insurance policies.

As the old year gave way to the new, the MIA dug in for the long haul. Its talks with the city commissioners and bus company officials had been unsuccessful, and on 12 January 1956 its board voted to continue the boycott indefinitely. Any romance had been replaced by a steely determination to see the boycott through to the bitter end, and such resolve was necessary in the face of threats upon the persons and livelihoods of supporters. Not only were white employers encouraged to desist from helping their staff get to work, they were also encouraged to dismiss those taking part in the boycott. On 21 January, Mayor Gayle met with three low-profile, non-MIA African-American clergymen, and together they announced to Montgomery's newspapers that a settlement had been reached, and that it was acceptable for African Americans to resume taking buses. On hearing the news, M. L. and his colleagues moved swiftly to counter this misinformation, travelling every highway and byway to tell their fellow strikers that the boycott was still in place.

INTIMIDATION

This turn of events further vexed the white power brokers, who stepped up their campaign of intimidation. On 26 January 1956, M. L. was arrested for speeding; he was purportedly driving at thirty miles an hour in a twenty-five mile an hour zone. To add insult to injury, he was slapped in a grimy jail in a deserted part of town. His supporters were alerted to the situation and Ralph Abernathy promptly arrived to bail him. While the arrest was M. L.'s first real jail experience, his incarceration revealed that he was being singled out for special treatment in the belief that the body of the organization could not survive without the head.

The jail experience, coupled with the pressures of leadership, and a spate of threatening telephone calls to his parsonage, brought M. L. to a crisis point on the evening of 27 January 1956. After receiving one particularly nasty late-night hate call, an insomnia-plagued M. L. broke down at his dining table. He made a cup of coffee, which he nursed while mulling over ways in which he could make a dignified retreat from Montgomery and the pressures caused by the bus boycott. With a mind in turmoil he turned to God in prayer, where he acknowledged his limitations and his over-reliance on his earthly father, rather than his heavenly one. It was while in prayer that his epiphany occurred, and in his own words: "... I could hear an inner voice saying to me, 'Martin Luther, stand up for righteousness. Stand up for justice. Stand up for truth. And I will be with you, even until the end of the world' ... I heard the voice of Jesus saying still fight on..."

Such divine intervention proved vital, as four days later his parsonage was firebombed. Although M. L. was attending a weekly church meeting at

the time, Coretta and baby Yolanda were at home when the bombers struck. While no one was hurt, M. L. returned home to comfort his family and calm the agitated supporters who had encircled his house. The previous night's spiritual revelations also enabled him to soothe a fretful Daddy King when he arrived from Montgomery to implore his son to step aside from the boycott and return home. Further literal trials were to follow. On 21 February he was forced to abandon lectures to students at Fisk University in Nashville, Tennessee, to scuttle back to Montgomery to face charges, alongside eighty boycott leaders, of conspiracy to interfere with lawful business. M. L. was summarily tried and convicted, and ordered to pay $500 plus costs or serve 386 days in a penal institution. Even though the MIA's coffers had been stretched by the boycott, supporters came to his aid with financial donations. (The MIA had been forced to meet repairs on carpool vehicles, travel-related costs, and other outgoings linked to the boycott.)

The boycott also created tensions between M. L. and the local chapter of the NAACP over the former claiming much of the credit and limelight for local events. The NAACP hierarchy in New York, under the able but often-pompous leadership of Roy Wilkins, was quietly vexed at the MIA's actions, which interfered with its well-choreographed attempts to use the law to challenge segregation. This tense situation was compounded by E. D. Nixon's involvement in the boycott; he headed the local branch of the NAACP and initially held the role of MIA treasurer. The events in Montgomery escalated M. L. to national prominence, leading to an increased number of lucrative speaking engagements. This, alongside other fund-raising activities, bolstered MIA reserves, but also engendered accusations of financial wrongdoing. Individuals with a vendetta accused M. L. of misusing funds to purchase new cars, and MIA staff of being profligate in their stewardship of finances. Of the three so-called "great vices", money, sex, and power, M. L. was undoubtedly susceptible to sex. However, any critical study of him reveals a man who was never motivated by material gain. The writer Michael Eric Dyson points to M. L. as being "extraordinarily scrupulous about his finances", giving the "movement most of his income, including the more than $200,000 he earned in annual speaking fees". Dyson also points out that M. L.'s initial reluctance to own a house and take out suitable life insurance proved a bone of contention with Coretta.[9] He would later become a student of Mahatma Gandhi, which resulted in him viewing materialism as a hindrance to his spiritual and psychological development.

M. L.'s growing interest in Gandhi had been a result of conversations with Glen A. Smiley and Bayard Rustin in late February 1956. Smiley was a middle-aged white Texan-born minister who had been a conscientious objector during the Second World War. As a student of non-violence, Smiley had taken an interest in M. L.'s early pronouncements about the MIA's

Bayard Rustin, the gifted civil rights activist and advisor to Martin Luther King, speaks during a press conference.

non-violent approach toward the bus boycott. By contrast, Rustin was a dapper, black Pennsylvania-born Quaker with left-wing sympathies and a curious penchant for speaking like a West Indian aristocrat. Rustin was also a homosexual and had been arrested for "lewd" activities in California in the 1950s. Both Smiley and Rustin were part of the Fellowship for Reconciliation, or FOR (Rustin would part company with FOR over his sexuality), and they arrived in Montgomery that February to add intellectual gravitas and a non-violent grounding to the boycott. Both men were impressed by M. L., but surprised at his preparedness to use armed guards to protect his parsonage. Rustin would later rebuke the non-violent M. L. for keeping a loaded pistol at his home, and for "his almost casual attitude to guns". Smiley left M. L. several books on Gandhi, and was later to wax lyrical to colleagues that "[M.L.] had been called by God for such work and that he could become the [African American] version of Gandhi".

The boycott continued, with both sides hardening their positions, until on 13 November 1956 the United States Supreme Court declared that "Alabama's state and local laws requiring segregation were unconstitutional". The court's judgment took over a month to take effect, meaning the boycott lasted over a year. M. L. and his supporters would be some of the first African Americans to board Montgomery's desegregated buses in early December 1956.

This was undoubtedly a triumph for Montgomery's African-American community and the MIA leadership in particular. It also cemented M. L.'s position as one of the country's foremost spokespersons on civil rights – a remarkable feat for someone still in his mid twenties. But while M. L.'s star was in the ascendancy, dark clouds hovered. The MIA's victory resulted in the customary white racist backlash of bombings, beatings, and death threats. While it would be wrong to describe the boycott as a pyrrhic victory, it came at a great cost to M.L.'s well-being. The pressures of leadership and the near constant media attention gave rise to a melancholy that would never fully leave him.

M. L. was now a national figure, and it appeared inconceivable that a man who only the previous year had been a preacher in a prestigious but local church could return to such a parochial position. He would later claim that he never wanted to lead any campaign; yet there was undoubtedly a need for someone to take on the role. It was a case of cometh the hour, cometh the man.

Chapter 4
THE TIMES THEY ARE A-CHANGING

As the victors of a hard won campaign, M. L. and the MIA served to inspire a generation of church and community leaders to challenge bus segregation in their towns and cities, fully cognizant that a unified African-American stance had every probability of being triumphant. According to M. L., Montgomery had spawned "A courageous new Negro with a sense of 'somebodiness' and self-respect, and ... a new determination to achieve freedom and human dignity no matter what the cost."[1] With the boycott at an end, M. L. was uncertain about which direction both he and the MIA should take. Although African Americans could ride on buses without any concern over seating arrangements, there were many establishments in the city that still denied them access.

In January 1957 around sixty African-American leaders, most of whom were clergy, met at Daddy King's church in Atlanta for discussions which led to the formation of the Southern Leaders Conference, a region-wide equivalent of the MIA. This new entity took its place alongside the National Urban League (NUL), a conservative organization founded in 1911 to "enable African Americans to secure economic self-reliance, parity, power and civil rights".[2] Other "race" organizations included the Congress of Racial Equality (CORE), which was established by two white students and African-American scholar, James L. Farmer. CORE's leaders were "deeply influenced by Henry David Thoreau and the teachings of Gandhi and the non-violent civil disobedience campaign that he used successfully against British rule in India". Towering over all these groups was the NAACP, the largest and oldest civil rights-based organization in the USA. Its head, Roy Wilkins, who had been wary of M. L.'s leadership of the MIA, was most alarmed on hearing about the formation of the Southern Leaders Conference.

At a second Southern Leaders Conference meeting on 14 February 1957 in New Orleans, M. L. was voted leader, and the organization inserted the term "Christian" to become the Southern Christian Leadership Conference – more commonly known as the SCLC. The addition of "Christian" would highlight the Christian ideals of love and reconciliation, and offset accusations of communism and unAmerican activities. Moreover, by linking the SCLC to the church, the members hoped this would display black self-determination, agency, and leadership.

Key to all these developments was Bayard Rustin, whose working papers spoke of fighting segregation by means of non-violent "direct action" – boycotts, street demonstrations, and any other means "except lawsuits". Alongside Rustin was Stanley Levison, a wealthy Jewish New York attorney who had raised funds in support of the Montgomery bus boycott. Levison was a known left-wing sympathizer (his detractors denounced him as a communist and argued that both he and Rustin revealed the real "red" agenda of the civil rights movement). The third member of this triumvirate was Ella Baker, a Virginia-born African-American woman for whom the term "feisty" was invented. Miss Baker, as she preferred to be called (despite the fact that she was briefly married to a clergyman), had experienced a near lifetime's worth of activism by the time she became involved in the SCLC. This Northern clique would play a key role in the direction of the SCLC, leading to arguments that "non-Christian outsiders" were dominating the organization. Although the organization was supposedly Southern in its focus, its ambitions were not limited by geography, and one of M. L.'s first proposals was to lead a "Prayer Pilgrimage to Washington" to coincide with the third anniversary of the Brown Education decision. After taking advice from Rustin and Levison, M. L. also announced a "Crusade for Citizenship" – a voter registration drive in the South. Both SCLC programmes raised the hackles of the already territorial Roy Wilkins, whose NAACP had been excluded from initial SCLC meetings to discuss these campaigns. Relations between the two were not helped by M. L.'s criticisms of the NAACP's "needless fights in the lower courts", and it took the intervention of the veteran activist A. Philip Randolph to persuade the NAACP to partake in the "Prayer Pilgrimage".

As it was, around 20,000 people gathered at Washington's Lincoln Memorial in May 1957 to hear M. L. deliver the keynote address at the Pilgrimage. Once again, he showed an expectant, largely African-American crowd that he had few peers as an orator. Like all great public speakers, he possessed the adroitness to move an audience, and that spring day he played on the emotions of his listeners like a maestro performing with a Stradivarius. He used the timbre of his wonderful voice to deliver words of hope that took his audience to the lofty heights of rapture. Yet at the appropriate moment, he punctuated proceedings with a

A large crowd gathers at Washington's Lincoln Memorial for the "Prayer Pilgrimage" in May 1957 to hear Martin Luther King speak about the need for greater government action on civil rights.

THE TIMES THEY ARE A-CHANGING

dash of sobering reality and angst that made even the hardest of men reach for their handkerchiefs. By the end of his speech the crowd resembled his church congregation, nodding and affirming almost every word he uttered. He walked away with the plaudits – much to the chagrin of Wilkins and others, who denounced the pilgrimage as M. L.'s "ego trip".

CRUSADE FOR CITIZENSHIP

The other big SCLC project, the "Crusade for Citizenship", sought to double the numbers of African Americans registered to vote in the South. The seasoned activist Ella Baker moved from her native New York to the SCLC's new headquarters in Atlanta, to work as acting director on this huge, ambitious project. Baker's initial task involved raising $200,000 to fund mass meetings in twenty-one cities, which would coincide with the anniversary of President Abraham Lincoln's birthday on 12 February 1958. Baker would find her efforts stymied as a result of a lack of funds (she initially had no office out of which to work, and few support staff), poor strategic planning, local politicking, and the stubbornness of the SCLC's male leadership. Baker had planned a mass movement that would empower the grass roots and "assist in the sharing of resources and experiences". However, she found that the resources to carry out voter registration activities never matched M. L.'s flowing oratory. What added to Baker's frustration was M. L.'s refusal to give real authority to her, despite him being occupied with a range of leadership activities. In Baker's opinion, this was due to her gender and lack of clerical status. Baker for her part refused to acquiesce to the "Great Leader", leading to tensions between the two. Her work was also compounded by grass roots supporters who thought more emphasis should be placed on the desegregation of schools and public facilities rather than a protracted voters' campaign. Her efforts were also not helped by the enactment of a Civil Rights Act in 1957 (albeit a toothless one), and President Eisenhower's intervention with US paratroopers to desegregate the Central High School in Little Rock, Arkansas. These developments encouraged many would-be activists to side with the NAACP's legal approach rather than the SCLC's campaign. Wilkins moved to distance the NAACP from the SCLC's campaign and privately reproached M. L. over his attempts to recruit NAACP stalwart Medgar Evers to his campaign. Despite his obvious displeasure with M. L., Wilkins was mindful of publicly criticizing his would-be rival for fear of ruining the new-found black unity.

M. L.'s public stock was on the rise, and in March 1957 Ghana's soon-to-be leader, Kwame Nkrumah, invited him and Coretta to West Africa to mark his country's independence from Britain. M. L.'s first visit to Africa provided a great opportunity to draw links between the civil rights movement in the US and the growing anti-colonial feeling on the African continent. Vice-President Richard Nixon was the USA's most senior representative in Ghana and, at an independence-related function, M. L. upbraided his administration for its slowness in supporting the civil rights movement.[3] M. L. took the opportunity to invite Nixon to Alabama, "Where [African Americans] are seeking the same kind of freedom Ghana is celebrating."

On 17 June, M. L. and Abernathy travelled to Washington for their meeting with Nixon, which proved cordial but far from conclusive, with the cautious and contradictory vice-president ruling out a presidential

John F. Kennedy sits while
Vice-President Richard M.
Nixon reads his notes as both
prepare for a live television
debate during the 1960 US
election campaigns.

visit to the South. M. L. did manage to extract the concession of a Nixon fact-finding visit to either New Orleans or Atlanta. The meeting with Nixon convinced M. L. that he needed to remain politically impartial while attempting to eke out concessions for African-American rights. While he had voted Republican at the previous election he remained guarded about his political affiliations, ensuring they were secondary to his civil rights work.

In between administering his SCLC duties, speaking engagements, and pastoral activities, M. L. set about writing his account of the victorious

Montgomery bus boycott. The resulting book, *Stride Toward Freedom*, which was published in September 1958, was as much M. L.'s work as it was Stanley Levison's, with flourishes from Bayard Rustin. (This approach would be typical of nearly all his books and writings, which were a miscellany of his ideas, fused with those of others.) That same month he stood trial on charges of loitering outside a courthouse. He had been arrested while attempting to enter the courthouse to hear a case involving Ralph Abernathy, who had been assaulted for allegedly cavorting with his assailant's wife. M. L. was found guilty of "refusing to obey an officer", and repudiated the $14 fine for what he regarded as trumped-up charges. After a blaze of publicity, the Montgomery police commissioner decided to pay the fine.

Later that month, while signing copies of his book in Blumstein's department store in Harlem, a deranged middle-aged African-American woman, Izola Ware Curry, stabbed him with a sharpened letter opener. Photographs of the would-be assassination show a calm-looking M. L. with the seven-inch weapon protruding from his chest. While recovering in a nearby hospital, he was told by his surgeons that a sneeze would have proved fatal. The stabbing heightened M. L.'s martyr complex and, like his heroes Jesus Christ and Gandhi, he believed that he would be killed as a result of his work.

M. L. spent the latter months of 1958 recuperating from his injuries and playing with Martin Luther King III, who had been born the previous year on 23 October 1957. While convalescing he received an offer to visit India, the home of his hero, Gandhi. Such were the constraints of his diary, M. L. believed that if he postponed the visit he would probably never get a similar

★★★★ FINAL

SUNDAY NEWS
NEW YORK'S PICTURE NEWSPAPER ®

 10¢

Vol. 38. No. 21   Copr. 1958 News Syndicate Co. Inc.   New York 17, N.Y., Sunday, September 21, 1958*   WEATHER: Rain, mild.

MARTIN LUTHER KING STABBED

A Letter Opener in His Chest, the Rev. Martin Luther King has wounded hand treated by Nettie Carter Jackson, of Brooklyn, at W. 123d St. police station. Leader of bus boycott by Negroes in Montgomery, Ala., was stabbed by woman as he autographed copies of his book in Harlem store. —*Story on page 3*

A calm-looking Martin Luther King sits while his wounded hand is dressed. A deranged woman stabbed King in the chest with a letter opener while he was signing books. The blade can be seen protruding from King's white shirt.

"... the strongest bond of fraternity was the common cause of minority and colonial peoples in America, Africa and Asia struggling to throw off racialism and imperialism."

opportunity to see the spiritual home of the non-violence movement. Prior to visiting India, M. L. had admitted to the Reverend Glen Smiley that he knew little about Gandhi's ideas, and unlike many of his African-American contemporaries such as Bayard Rustin, Mordecai Johnson, and James Lawson, he had never spent any time in India, studying the principles of non-violent political action.

In February 1959, M. L., Coretta, and MIA colleague and biographer Dr Lawrence D. Reddick boarded a New York plane for Paris, arriving in Delhi, India on 10 February for a thirty-day tour. In truth, India was as pleased to see M. L. as he was to visit the country. The Indians had followed the Montgomery bus boycott, especially after M. L. mentioned Gandhi and Indian independence. According to M. L., "We were looked upon as brothers with the colour of our skins as something of an asset ... But the strongest bond of fraternity was the common cause of minority and colonial peoples in America, Africa and Asia struggling to throw off racialism and imperialism." The Indian break gave him a first-hand opportunity to learn more about the man he considered an icon, and the architect of *Satyagraha*, or soul force, which, according to Gandhi, "is the vindication of truth not by infliction of suffering on the opponent but on one's self".[4] M. L. used his visit to share his views on the "race" question with university students, and he explored the topic of non-violence with various heads of state, including Prime Minister Jawaharlal Nehru and Vice-President Sarvepalli Radhakrishnan, who was also a noted philosopher. Prime Minister Nehru spoke at length about his country's efforts to proscribe (Hindu) caste discrimination against the "Untouchables", or Dalits, as they are now known. Had M. L. been able to make the visit a few years earlier, he would

have heard another side of the caste discrimination story from Dr Bhimrao Ramji Ambedkar, who was a champion for Dalit rights, and arguably his direct equivalent in India. Dr Ambedkar, who died in 1956, remained highly critical of all Indian political parties, and even Gandhi, over their perennial neglect of the country's large minority.

M. L. left India "more convinced than ever before that non-violent resistance was the most potent weapon available to oppressed people in their struggle for freedom". He immediately launched into a round of speaking engagements looking to generate funds to pour into the SCLC's moribund coffers. Although travel had broadened his mind, his absences did little to assist the running of the SCLC. Its voter registration efforts proved far from effective and had accrued only a fraction of the people envisaged, and its Institute of Nonviolent Resistance to Segregation failed to ignite the imagination of would-be supporters. Even the involvement of the dynamic James Lawson, a contemporary of M. L., had failed to spark these non-violence workshops into life.

Martin Luther King and Coretta
talk with Prime Minister Jawaharlal
Nehru during the Kings' one-month
visit to India.

By 1959, it had become apparent to M. L. that it was impossible to pastor a church in Montgomery, Alabama, and run an organization in Atlanta, Georgia: something had to give. As someone who took real pride in his Christian ministry, M. L. was increasingly embarrassed by the quality of leadership he was providing at Dexter. Although his congregation never openly complained, church records reveal that he was more often away than present on Sundays, and when he was in the pulpit, his sermons lacked the preparation that characterized his preaching of earlier years. M. L. had too much integrity and respect for his congregation to continue offering such substandard fare, and after discussions with Levison, Rustin and Daddy King, he resolved to leave Dexter and resume pastoral duties at his father's church in Atlanta. His return home would give him ample opportunity to devote his energies to revitalizing the flagging SCLC. A tearful M. L. told his far-from-surprised congregation about his decision during a sermon in November 1959 – there had been rumours of his imminent departure throughout that year, and although they were sad to lose the now world-famous preacher, most congregants knew he had outgrown both Dexter and Montgomery.

At the start of a new decade, M. L., Coretta and the growing King family returned to Atlanta, the city he knew as home. Daddy King was only too pleased to see his son return, having never wanted him to leave in the first place. Despite the fact that Daddy King had become a born-again civil rights crusader, partly as a result of his son's activities, he was at pains to inform Atlanta's establishment that M. L. did not plan to "create any trouble in the city, but was coming home to preach". What Daddy King failed to acknowledge was that by 1960, M. L. had stopped being Daddy King's son;

Arm-in-arm: Martin Luther King leads a civil rights march which includes (from left to right) Ralph Abernathy, James Forman, Martin Luther King, Jesse Douglas, and John Lewis.

rather Daddy King was the father of the world-famous Reverend Dr Martin Luther King Jr. M. L. was now his own man; and while his close friends may have still called him "M. L." or "Mike", to most Americans, and the wider world, the name "Martin Luther King" denoted the youthful, world-famous civil rights leader, not an ageing Ebenezer pastor.

Martin Luther King Jr's return to Atlanta did little to quell the rivalries between the SCLC and NAACP. His public affirmations and statements about the distinctiveness of the respective organizations tended to contradict his actions. In 1961 he turned down a discreet offer to become an NAACP board member, citing diary and scheduling commitments as an excuse. The continuing spats between the NAACP and SCLC only served to alienate young, restless African Americans who were rapidly losing faith in the NAACP's court-related approach, and the SCLC's fixation with voter registration. Many were students at black universities and colleges in the South, and they wanted to see more of the direct action that had brought about change in Montgomery in 1955–56. Being savvy, and not too long out of college himself, King was aware of these youthful aspirations, but he struggled to find ways in which the SCLC could satisfy these often fiery ambitions. Paradoxically, it was the veteran Ella Baker who would play a key role in the establishment of what would become the premier student movement, the Student Nonviolent Coordinating Committee (SNCC) – pronounced "snick".

The SNCC established its headquarters in Atlanta, with King providing seed money for office space and equipment. Despite this assistance, the SNCC aimed to be an independent entity with links to both the SCLC's youth wing and the NAACP's youth councils, thus giving it impartiality.

And similar to the SCLC, the SNCC adopted non-violence as its raison d'être. Its first chair was the Fisk graduate student Marion Barry, who would later become the controversial mayor of Washington DC. Barry was supported by activists such as Julian Bond, Diane Nash, James Bevel (the dynamic Nash and the mercurial Bevel would later marry), John Lewis (currently a US congressman), and Bernard Lafayette.

King's return to Atlanta coincided with the student-inspired non-violent sit-ins at the Woolworth's department store in Greensboro, North Carolina, where a handful of students occupied the white-only seats at the store's lunch counter. Despite being summarily refused service by staff, they refused to vacate their seats. Over the following weeks, students such as Nashville-based Cordy Tindell (C. T.) Vivian, Diane Nash, James Bevel, and Bernard Lafayette stepped up the attack on Woolworth's whites-only seating policy by organizing sit-ins at other department stores across the South. What began in a department store would spread to "other places of public accommodation – movie theatres ... public libraries, courtroom seating and full-service restaurants".[5] The sit-ins not only emboldened the students, they led to an African-American student-based protest movement that would transform the modus operandi of the civil rights movement. According to the historian David Reynolds, "they [the students] were of a different generation, impatient with the incrementalism and compromise of older blacks. Offspring of the new black middle class, aroused and often radicalised by higher education, they were now ready to take the initiative. In the early 1960s it was often the young who led and the black leaders who followed."[6]

The students undoubtedly showed apathetic or sceptical African Americans, especially adults, that they could be agents of change. On a deeper level, the sit-ins empowered those who had been cowed by decades, if not centuries, of white supremacy, and exposed the myth that change could only take place after protracted legal battles in the courts. The sit-in movement completely cut across the NAACP's legal approach to bringing

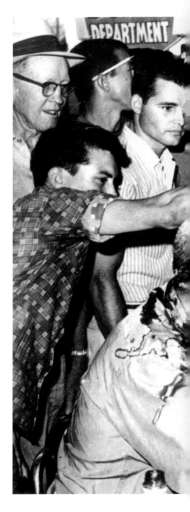

Black and white students face the fury of Southern racists as they try to integrate a segregated café bar.

change, and it can be argued that it spelled the death knell for Wilkins' organization among African-American students. The sit-in movement proved a fillip for the SNCC and its key organizer, Ella Baker. She had become disillusioned with what she deemed the SCLC's ego-obsessed, chauvinistic leadership, and regarded the student movement as non-hierarchical in nature, and less male dominated.

While King was keen to utilize the dynamism of students, other matters preoccupied his return to Atlanta, particularly those which followed him from Montgomery. In February 1960, he was arrested on two criminal counts of perjury, referring to the accuracy of his tax returns for 1956 and 1958. Although King had paid $1,600 in back taxes, Alabama's power brokers were determined to "get King", and charged him with perjury on a tax return – the first time in the history of the state. As the journalist and writer Louis E. Lomax pointed out, "false rumours abounded about King's largesse and misappropriation of funds; big house, fancy cars and fine clothes", and the subsequent court case questioned his integrity. In May, an all-white jury found him not guilty; he was one of the few African Americans to obtain justice from such an ethnic make-up. His brushes with the law continued later that year when he was charged with driving with the wrong licence. He had failed to transfer his Alabama driver's licence to Georgia, and in September 1960 was fined $25 and placed on a year's probation.

Mindful that the SCLC would never achieve its full potential without the appropriate finance and staff, King not only looked to enhance his number of revenue-raising speaking engagements, he also increased staff numbers. He employed Massachusetts-born preacher and civil rights activist Reverend Wyatt Tee Walker as the SCLC's executive director.

Right: The Reverend Wyatt Tee Walker preaches.

Below: Andrew Young takes part in a press conference with Martin Luther King.

Walker was a flamboyant character whose brilliance was matched only by his alleged ego and vanity. When King subsequently commented that he possessed "one of the keenest minds of the nonviolent revolution" he failed to mention his adminstrative prowess, tactical nous, and media savvy. Yet, for all his brilliance, the fact that Walker was both male and clergy meant he avoided the recalcitrant chauvinism faced by his immediate predecessor, Ella Baker. Walker and his newly installed team of Dorothy Cotton and James R. Wood set about the arduous task of reorganizing the SCLC's activities, beginning with fund-raising.

King also brought on board Andrew Young, an urbane, educated clergyman from New Orleans who had spent time working for the National Council of Churches in New York. Young, who was also a disciple of Gandhian non-violence and active in voter registration work, would become a firm friend of King, and his measured approach, tact, and charm appeared to single him out as a potential SCLC leader if anything happened to the existing one.

The other major event overshadowing the second half of 1960 was the battle for the White House between the Republican candidate and US vice-president Richard M. Nixon, and his youthful Democratic opponent John F. Kennedy. Looking to take advantage of the heightened interest in the elections, King and A. Philip Randolph proposed a mass march on the Republican and Democractic conventions that July. While the NAACP and Urban League remained cool toward the proposal, Congressman Adam Clayton Powell took umbrage with the march, accusing King of being under the influence of his "socialist" special assistant Bayard Rustin and fund-raiser Stanley Levison. Powell upped the stakes by calling on King to fire Rustin or face exposure of a homosexual nature. Disturbed by this turn of events, King consulted colleagues, who encouraged him to face down Powell's brazen extortion. King opted for prevarication, forcing Rustin to tender his resignation, with the expectation that his boss would reject it and offer him his unconditional support. In an act that his comrade A. J. Muste described as "cowardly", King accepted Rustin's resignation, but agreed that his former strategist could continue in an unpaid, untenured capacity.

As the election approached, King was eager to find out where both presidential candidates stood on civil rights. He had met Nixon after Ghana, but remained wary of Eisenhower's administration, which was accused of "showing little sympathy for civil rights ... rural poverty and urban decay".[7] Unlike previous Republican presidents, "Ike", as he was often called, could no longer rely on the default vote of African Americans for "Lincoln's Party", as President Franklin Delano Roosevelt's reforms during the 1930s economic downturn resulted in the defection of many black people to the Democrats. John F. Kennedy (or JFK), Nixon's opponent, wanted to bask in

Roosevelt's glory, positing himself as a man with similar "new leadership for a new era".

Notwithstanding his seemingly progressive appearance, it is said that by the late 1950s, the only African Americans JFK knew were chauffeurs, valets, or domestics. And in a moment of candour during the run-up to the 1960 US elections, he confessed to a black dentist: "I don't know five Negroes of your calibre well enough to call them by their first names."[8] More importantly, from a political standpoint it was argued that "[Kennedy] could not empathise ... with pains felt by African Americans".[9] His biographer, Robert Dallek, has suggested that JFK's "response to the great civil rights debates of 1957–1960 was largely motivated by self-serving political considerations".[10] Like many Northern-based Democrats, Kennedy remained fearful of losing the support of his staunch segregationist counterparts in the South, and on several occasions civil rights activists such as Roy Wilkins accused him of "rubbing political elbows" with Southern (Democrat) segregationists.

In the run-up to the election, Kennedy appeared to show a clearer commitment to civil rights, and in mid June 1960 he had a breakfast meeting with King which enabled him to outline his "manifesto" on the issue. His apparent new-found commitment to civil rights, coupled with his eloquence and charm, appeared to win over a doubting King. Kennedy would subsequently describe civil rights as a "moral question", promising both legislation and executive action to improve the lot of African Americans, especially with regard to government jobs. His campaign also spent "thousands of dollars on free pullout sections inserted in black newspapers ... which featured rows of photographs showing Kennedy alongside blacks such

Presidential candidate Senator
John F. Kennedy, on the
campaign trail during the 1960
US elections.

as Congressman Dawson, Ghana's Minister of Finance ... and his own secretary Virginia Battle".[11]

What arguably clinched the African-American vote for JFK was King's arrest and detention that autumn for violating the terms of his earlier probation for driving around Georgia with his Alabama driving licence. (King had been arrested with students at an Atlanta department store lunch counter.) He was initially placed in an Atlanta jail, but was later transferred to a state prison, leading to mass publicity. A combination of genuine concern and naked political opportunism encouraged Kennedy to take the unprecedented step of calling Coretta to register his concern and offer assistance. Although a tacit agreement between all parties kept this intervention out of the national media, African-American clergymen took this as a sign of the

Democrat's commitment to civil rights, and endorsed JFK from their pulpits. Daddy King, who was a lifelong Republican, spoke openly about switching allegiance to the Democrats, despite "Kennedy being a Catholic". Indeed, the November presidential elections proved to be a close-run contest, in which the African-American vote was vital. The telegenic JFK polled 49.7 per cent to Nixon's 49.5 per cent of the popular vote. However, JFK gained a huge 70 per cent of the African-American vote, but lost support among white Southerners who were concerned over his support for civil rights.

The presidential election did not thwart the activities of students who continued their sit-ins across the South. By the following year, CORE's James Farmer spoke about mobilizing the sit-ins, and in March 1961 he gained the SCLC's and SNCC's support for bus journeys into the Deep South aimed at desegregating their public facilities. What became known as the Freedom Rides began in May 1961, with black and white "Freedom Riders" travelling south in two buses from Washington DC, passing through South Carolina, Georgia, and Alabama with the intention of reaching New Orleans. Farmer and his volunteers knew the inherent dangers of such an enterprise, and one of the buses was duly firebombed in Anniston, Alabama. It was later attacked by a mob of racists in Birmingham, resulting in two students being badly beaten. The Greyhound and Trailways bus companies subsequently refused to transport the group any further, forcing them to take a plane to New Orleans.

The second bus faced similar problems in Montgomery, Alabama. On 20 May around 1,000 white toughs met the bus and were able to run amok in the absence of any police. Those injured included the head of *Time-Life*'s news bureau, Norman Ritter, JFK's special representative, John

Siegenthaler, and the SNCC's John Lewis. On hearing the news, King sped off to offer support. He soon found himself holed up in a Montgomery church with James Farmer and 1,500 others, while a baying mob encircled the building. King was forced to call Attorney General Robert Kennedy to alert him to the situation and demand help. A reluctant Bobby Kennedy acquiesced, and sent hundreds of federal marshals to bring order to the mounting chaos. Later that day, a fired-up King dispensed with his usual measured approach and spoke with real anger about the violence meted out against those who wanted to test whether the South had embraced the growing clamour for change. King also complained about the dearth of protection offered to the Freedom Riders, which he interpreted as Kennedy's reluctance to take desegregation efforts seriously. That evening King and the Attorney General shared a heated telephone conversation, during which Bobby Kennedy stated that King must not make "statements that sound like a threat [as] .. That's not the way to deal with us."[12]

A casually dressed Robert F. Kennedy, the US Attorney General, makes a call from his office to keep abreast of security issues surrounding the Freedom Riders' bus campaign.

Even though King was firm in his condemnation of the police and unequivocal in his support for the Freedom Riders, he still faced the ire of the more militant students who denounced him as a "proxy proteser", a man who spoke much about Gandhi, but did not share the great pandit's willingness to place himself at the forefront of danger alongside his suffering people. King responded by arguing that he had to stay out of jail to continue the wider civil rights work, and boost SCLC coffers via speaking engagements. Despite King's arguments, one writer has suggested that the "Freedom Rides ... marked a widening gap between King and the students, which grew into institutional rivalry between the SCLC and SNCC and raised deep and dangerous disagreements about the tactics and strategy of the movement..."[13]

Chapter 5
I HAVE A DREAM

There were even more changes in the King household in 1961. His second son, and third child, Dexter Scott (named after his former Montgomery church and Coretta's maiden name) was born on 30 January. And a growing family only increased the strain on the Kings' already pressurized marriage. As an international figure, King was frequently at speaking engagements, leaving Coretta to shoulder the burden of running the household. Friends of the family have disclosed that

Martin Luther King spends a rare moment relaxing with his daughter Yolanda and son Martin Luther King III.

she was unhappy with this situation, and suggestions that her husband had a "higher calling" to lead the civil rights movement proved crumbs of comfort. King was also aware that he was spending more time in motels and hotels (those catering for African Americans) than at home. The constant travel for fund-raising activities also meant King was unable to provide the SCLC with the strong, visionary leadership that would move the civil rights issue up the political agenda. King was also cognizant that the SCLC lacked a "moment of destiny or testing" such as the Montgomery Bus Boycott. Unlike the MIA, the SCLC had spent its relatively short time overseeing the worthy but dubiously effective voter registration crusade across the South. That was one of the reasons why King became very interested in Albany, a sleepy, segregated city in Georgia.

Albany was the largest city in Terrell County. Terrell's 26,000 African-American residents, who formed around a third of the population, called it "Terrible Terrell" because of its long history of crude and cruel forms of segregation and racism. Many of the city's younger black people were keen to see Terrell undergo the changes occurring in other parts of the South, and the arrival of SNCC members Charles Sherrod and Cordell Reagon in mid November 1961 to run workshops on non-violent direct action proved a stimulus. Similar to the Freedom Riders' strategy, Sherrod, Reagon, and their student supporters consequently carried out a sit-in at the Albany bus terminal to challenge transport segregation. While these SNCC actions did not result in the usual round of arrests, they generated national coverage, and by December 1961 King and the SCLC began to take an interest in the city.

Later that month, a number of local and competing civil rights groups came together to form the Albany Movement, with local doctor

The wily police chief Laurie
Pritchett halts a Martin Luther
King-led demonstration in Albany
in December 1961.

William Anderson installed as president, and real estate agent Slater
King (no relation) its vice-president. The Albany Movement sought to
use a multifaceted approach to tackle segregation in the city, especially
its transport facilities. The campaign deployed the usual round of sit-ins,
demonstrations, boycotts, and litigation, initially attracting large numbers
of African Americans across the age ranges and social classes. While such
demonstrations led to arrests, Albany's chief of police, the wily, media-savvy
Laurie Pritchett, ensured that his officers refrained from using strong-arm
tactics, resulting in a paucity of reports or photographs of bloodied, beaten
demonstrators.

With many in jail, bail monies exhausted and negotiations stalling, the Albany Movement's Dr Anderson pleaded with King to get directly involved. King duly arrived on 15 December, much to the chagrin of SNCC supporters, who were annoyed that some saw King and his staff as a black version of the Magnificent Seven who rode into town to rescue hapless towns-folk from Mayor Kelley and his henchmen. It was during this period that some SNCC supporters began lampooning King as "De Lawd" or referring to him as "Slick". King's arrival duly brought with it the national media, and at a church-based meeting on the evening of 15 December, he fired up a full congregation with a talk about ending injustice and suffering. Media interest increased after King, Abernathy and other protesters were arrested the following day "for parading without a permit and obstructing the sidewalk". King and Abernathy were jailed in nearby Americus, where both refused bail or to pay fines if charged. King declared that he was prepared to spend Christmas in prison until some agreement had been made to accommodate black objections. Abernathy was later bailed and returned to Atlanta, where alongside Wyatt Tee Walker he dedicated the SCLC's efforts to Albany.

Back in Albany, the situation began to deteriorate. While King languished in prison, leaders from Albany's fractious black community entered into dubious discussions with Chief Pritchett, apparently reaching a loose agreement around the formation of a biracial committee on desegregation and the release of jailed demonstrators. These accommodations were conditional on an end to the protests and King's immediate return to Atlanta. Never one to stand in the way of negotiations, King agreed to bail and swiftly left Albany. No sooner had he returned home than Chief Pritchett and his colleagues denied any such arrangements with the black community, leaving a wrong-footed King to explain the curious agreement. The press regarded this as a "stunning defeat" and a "loss of face" for King; if Montgomery was his zenith, Albany became his nadir.

King and Abernathy would return to Albany in July 1962 to face a fine or time in prison – they opted for the latter. Embarrassed by the previous turn of events, King once again promised to stay in jail and refused bail. Although he hoped that his imprisonment would bolster the movement and force through federal reforms, his time behind bars was once again short-lived, and on 12 July Chief Pritchett notified King and Abernathy that their bail had been paid by an "unidentified black man". Abernathy was later to joke, "I've been thrown out of lots of places in my day, but never before have I been thrown out of jail."

Once again at liberty, King launched a determined offensive against the segregation of public facilities, promising to "fill up the jails" and "turn Albany up-side down". Having denied King the oxygen of prison-time publicity, Chief Pritchett ensured that African-American protesters received little public sympathy for their demonstrations. He encouraged his officers to match non-violent protest with non-violent arrests. Pritchett's folksy way with words and overall charm (he claimed to have read King's books and studied Gandhi's ideas on non-violence) won over the media, making the SCLC and SNCC appear outside agitators in Pritchett's peaceful, law-abiding city. To make matters worse, the federal district judge, J. Robert Elliott, a JFK appointee and known segregationist, handed down a temporary injunction banning all protests in Albany.

When a protest by a large crowd of African Americans became violent and ended with stone-throwing, Chief Pritchett was later to ask reporters if they saw the "non violent rocks" hurled at his men. A shamefaced King was forced to apologize and suspend demonstrations. He spent the rest of his time in Albany visiting the city's black haunts extolling the virtues of non-violence to thoroughly disheartened citizens. Robbed of the chance to protest peacefully, the Albany Movement floundered and slowly ground to a halt. King returned home to lick his wounds, and Albany remained as segregated as ever.

King and the SCLC were to rue their time in Albany, and the escapades in that city went down as one of the low points of the civil rights movement. At the SCLC's sixth convention in Birmingham, Alabama, King sought to salvage a semblance of dignity by arguing that Albany's black population now "had a heightened sense of their rights". Yet, in his more candid moments he knew that the success of future campaigns would be dependent on improved tactical planning at SCLC headquarters, coupled with greater on-the-ground coordination and leadership. It was during this convention that a Nazi supporter hit King several times in the face while he delivered the keynote address on stage. King refused to shield his head from his attacker, who was eventually restrained; King later declined to press charges against his assailant.

Both the conference and King's pummelling were largely ignored by the media, who were more interested in the events taking place in Mississippi, where African-American student James Meredith was trying to register at the all-white University of Mississippi (known as "Ole Miss"). Meredith's initial attempts were met by rejection, and the hullabaloo surrounding his

Tear gas is used to break up a night-time riot by white students and segregationist supporters opposed to James Meredith's attempts to desegregate the University of Mississippi.

enrolment attracted media attention and racist thugs, forcing the Kennedy administration to intervene. The president's announcement of a court order to register Meredith at the university was followed by a riot on campus that left two dead and a good many injured. Finally, a reluctant Kennedy deployed the Military Police Battalion and units from the Mississippi National Guard to quell the disturbances and enforce the court order.

King took a keen interest in the Meredith case and welcomed the outcome of the university's desegregation. After the Albany reversal, he spent serious time analysing the reasons for the "defeat", and concluded that his form of non-violent civil disobedience was most efficacious when black protesters incited white racist violence, especially involving the police. Such a hostile response, if caught on camera, would create a crisis of national proportions and force federal intervention. King would later use the term "dramatize" in reference to the way his direct action campaigns would focus attention on segregation; the SCLC would apply these lessons in the following year's campaign in Birmingham, Alabama.

The Albany experience also revealed to King that JFK and his Attorney General brother were more "willing to trade justice for peace in Albany – or at least what the white community called peace". He also raised concerns that local FBI agents had been in league with racist law officers – often turning a blind eye to violence. Such a stinging denunciation brought him into conflict with John Edgar Hoover, the notorious director of the Federal Bureau of Investigation (FBI). Hoover had long been wary of King, accusing him of being everything from a communist stooge to a "boy with the sexual urges of a tomcat".[1] Hoover, who was infamous for keeping secret files on the rich and famous, had persuaded Attorney General Robert Kennedy to authorize wiretaps on King and his associates, which began in earnest during the first years of the Kennedy administration.

For the vast majority of African Americans, 1963 would be a historic year, as it marked the centenary of President Abraham Lincoln's Emancipation Proclamation, which had freed enslaved African Americans. Like many of his peers, King was eager to see the anniversary marked with

a symbolic event worthy of such an important date in US history, and he
said as much at a round of rallies he attended to mark the anniversary on
New Year's Day. A little later that month he gathered with colleagues in
Dorchester, West Georgia, to hear Wyatt Tee Walker outline his strategy
document, Project "C" (Confrontation), which summarized the approach
the SCLC would take for its next campaign in Birmingham, Alabama.

Birmingham was an iron and steel town whose population had grown
from 3,000 in 1880 to 130,000 in 1910 as a result of these heavy industries.

Such industrial development did not lead to similar political or social advancements for the city's African-American residents, who remained systematically deprived of the vote through discriminatory practices such as literacy tests and a poll tax. When King described Birmingham as "the most segregated city in America" he was drawing attention to the totally disenfranchised African-American community, which constituted 40 per cent of the city's 340,000 inhabitants. Birmingham was known to have an active and violent chapter of the Ku Klux Klan, whose incendiary violence

Left: Birmingham, Alabama, was a city known for its steel production throughout King's lifetime.

Below: Ku Klux Klan members take part in a ceremony.

against African Americans had given the city the name "Bombingham". The emergence of the city's civil rights movement coincided with the rise of Fred Shuttlesworth, a Baptist pastor and co-founder of the Alabama Christian Movement for Human Rights (ACMHR). After the local chapter of the NAACP was outlawed in Alabama, Shuttlesworth's organization stepped into the breach to take up the slack. Shuttlesworth, who survived

a Christmas Day bombing attempt in 1956, was a combative man whose charismatic leadership of the ACMHR led critics, both inside and outside the church, to denounce him as a "wildman with a martyr complex".[2] The preacher and activist had lobbied King to make his city a testbed for the revamped SCLC executive, which now included pastor and Freedom Rider veteran, C. T. Vivian, and the erratic but compelling James Bevel.

Drawing on the lessons of Albany, the SCLC decided to conduct a massive direct action campaign which attacked the city's segregated department stores. They would hit the merchants where they felt it most – in their pockets – and it was hoped that financial matters would concentrate the minds of Birmingham's lawmakers. The SCLC postponed the campaign until after local elections and the birth of King's fourth and last child, a daughter, Bernice Alberta, who was born on 28 March 1963. This meant the campaign would coincide with Easter, a lucrative time for store owners, and a spiritually significant one for those taking part in activities which Fred Shuttlesworth called "a moral witness to give our community a chance to survive".

Unlike Albany, the SCLC made sure it maintained control of the campaign, and worked in partnership with Shuttlesworth's ACMHR to avoid the organizational rivalry and confused leadership that characterized Albany. The need for clear lines of leadership and unity was paramount, as the SCLC was crossing swords with Birmingham's commissioner of public safety, the truculent, racist Theophilus Eugene Connor, known to locals as "Bull" Connor. Despite his media background, Connor lacked the tact of Albany's Chief Pritchett, preferring belligerence to diplomacy, leaving King to describe him as "a racist who prided himself on knowing how to handle the Negro and keep him in his place". The SCLC was counting on

Eugene "Bull" Connor, the belligerent commissioner of public safety, Birmingham, Alabama, in 1963.

Bull Connor reverting to violent type to give it a victory that could break the "back of segregation all over the nation".

On 3 April 1963, the day after the more dignified but equally segregationist Albert Boutwell defeated Bull Connor in the mayoral elections, the SCLC bandwagon rolled into town and launched a series of mass meetings, sit-ins, marches, and demonstrations of direct action. True to form, Bull Connor and his officers moved in and arrested hundreds of demonstrators, but, to the dismay of Wyatt Tee Walker, Connor's men avoided any heavy-handedness. A further blow came a few days later when a court order proscribed protests in the city. Ensconced with colleagues

A handcuffed Martin Luther King being led to a courthouse, following his arrest for participation in a student-led demonstration.

in his room at the black-owned Gaston Motel, King pondered his next move: whether to adhere to the injunction, or march that Good Friday, 10 April. Fresh in his mind was his failure to do so in Albany after a similar injunction, which essentially ended that campaign. Yet his participation would involve breaking the law and result in his arrest and incarceration. Some within the SCLC were at pains to inform him that he needed to be at liberty to not only lead the campaign, but raise funds to alleviate their straitened circumstances. After much group discussion, King retreated to his bedroom for prayer, only to return decked out in his jeans and boots – his marching garb. He would march and be arrested.

King's decision to march and break the law was part of an ongoing evolution. He had previously believed that non-violent direct action within a clear Christian framework would engender a Damascene conversion in white Southerners who considered themselves good Christians. The events in Albany convinced him that such an approach was erroneous. While he still believed in inner goodness and the possibility of change, he recognized that change was more likely to materialize via legal compulsion than moral persuasion. As a result, SCLC campaign tactics moved toward non-violent provocation as opposed to persuasion. Unlike the latter, the former's dramatization of segregation usually resulted in the type of violence that forced the government to intervene. This led critics to accuse King of encouraging violence to effect his stated aims. King would elucidate his ideas in his *Letter from Birmingham Jail*, which was a response to condemnation from local white Christian clergy, and he stated that "non-violent direct action seeks to create such a crisis and foster such a tension that a community which has constantly refused to negotiate is forced to confront the issue.

99

It seeks so to dramatize the issue that it can no longer be ignored." He would also argue that it was more important to obey a "higher law" than legal injunctions that were "unjust, undemocratic and [an] unconstitutional misuse of the legal process".

King's decision to march saw him join countless others in jail. With so many locked up, the Birmingham movement began to flounder. Although his arrest was news, his incarceration and the ongoing campaign were not headline material. This led to protester numbers dwindling as apathy, fear of losing jobs, and an apparent dislike of Fred Shuttlesworth set in. Even the fund-raising activities of celebrity supporters such as Harry Belafonte made little impact on bail money constraints. The campaign that King had so publicly headed was in crisis, and in danger of going the way of Albany.

When all seemed lost, King's crusade found its knight in shining armour in the form of the tall, eccentric James Bevel. Bevel had a penchant for donning overalls and Jewish skullcaps, and was regarded by some as a throwback to an Old Testament prophet. Aware that there was a lack of adults, he persuaded his colleagues that children and young people could fill this vacuum. He argued that they had no jobs to lose and few issues with personal rivalries. Bevel even quoted Scripture to reinforce his argument, using the verses "Suffer the little ones to come unto me, for such is the Kingdom of God" to justify their participation.[3] King was initially against such a move; he was fearful of exposing children to Bull Connor's brutality, and mindful of how it would look to the public at large. (Malcolm X would denounce him as "unmanly" and "cowardly" for putting children in the frontline of the campaign.)

Notwithstanding these objections, Bevel had his way, and the students left their schools in droves to gather at churches and centres. After being schooled in the basic tenets of non-violent direct action, they were let loose to march in the streets. By the end of 3 May almost 1,000 languished in prison, many of them not even teenagers. This new twist caught the imagination of supporters, and more importantly, it attracted the media. Such youthful black insubordination proved too much for Connor, and the cameras were on hand to witness his officers at their most bullish. Images of children corralled into a park where powerful water cannons were turned on them were flashed across the nation and the world. Photos of snarling Alsatian dogs unleashed on screaming children appeared in the newspapers, while magazines carried stills of black onlookers being clubbed by menacing-looking officers. Thousands were arrested and equal numbers were injured and hospitalized as a result of police brutality. One such victim was Fred Shuttlesworth, who was hospitalized after being battered about the face by a powerful water hose. Alabama was scandalized and America was shamed. In an era when African countries were throwing off the last vestiges of colonial rule, the United States, the so-called "land of the free", used Soviet-style strategies to deny its then largest minority its rights. A clearly embarrassed JFK sent in Assistant Attorney General Burke Marshall and his deputy, Joseph F. Dolan, to negotiate as the violence continued into the second week of May.

The ongoing protests and the resulting violence only served to drive even more folk away from Birmingham's department stores, and as the economic boycott began to bite, the (white) Senior Citizens' Council moved to end it. Much to Bull Connor's vexation, a meeting was called where the two sides agreed on desegregating downtown stores; this was to be followed by public facilities, and an increase in African-American employment opportunities. Mindful of the increasing violence and these apparent concessions, King agreed to call off further demonstrations. When a hospitalized Shuttlesworth heard about his decision he discharged himself and confronted King about the wisdom of the truce. Using what could only be described as "industrial language" he accused King of selling out the campaign and demanded that it should continue. Shuttlesworth eventually relented, swayed in some part by King's feted diplomacy and the prospect of him getting to announce the news of the settlement to the press. Although the agreed concessions were far from earth-shattering (no agreement was reached on dropping the charges against the 2,500 arrested). King claimed Birmingham as "the most magnificent victory for justice we've ever seen in the South". What was all the more remarkable was that this "victory" had been achieved in just over seven weeks.

As always, a racist version of Newton's third law of motion occurred, with the reaction taking the form of bombings and Ku Klux Klan vigilante activities. The Gaston Motel, King's base in Birmingham, was bombed, as was the parsonage of his brother, A. D. King. Each bombing drew a newly empowered African-American community onto the streets to wage war with Bull Connor's officers. King was forced to return to the city to appeal for calm and a recommitment to non-violence.

The Birmingham campaign proved a boon for SCLC finances and a shot in the arm for the civil rights movement. For King it was a remarkable reversal of fortunes; in just over a year he went from being a loser in Albany to an all-round hero. He had taken on the "best of the worst" and had prevailed via non-violent direct action. Birmingham had demonstrated that America was changing. In Alabama, the staunch segregationist governor, George Wallace, who on taking up office in January 1963 proclaimed "segregation now, segregation tomorrow, segregation forever", was forced to step aside from the doorway of the University of Alabama and allow the admittance of two African-American students. Deputy Attorney General Nicholas Katzenbach, assisted by federal marshals, had forced the belligerent Wallace to accede to a federal court order. It appeared as if the Kennedy administration had finally located its moral compass on civil rights. Soon after facing down Wallace in Mississippi, President Kennedy appeared on television to address the nation on the civil rights issue. In a speech that at times verged on the passionate he stated: "We are confronted primarily with a moral issue ... It is as old as the scriptures and as clear as the American Constitution..." The rest of his address outlined America's need to enact laws that recognized black rights.

The following day, 12 June 1963, Medgar Evers, a D-Day war veteran and active civil rights campaigner, was slain in Mississippi by Ku Klux Klan killers. As with the murder of the teenager Emmett Till, also in that state, Evers' killing gained national prominence, highlighting both the sheer barbarity of aspects of Southern life and the need for legislation promoting African Americans' rights. Buoyed by the groundswell surrounding Evers' killing and the events in Birmingham, the president announced the most far-reaching civil rights bill in the USA's history on 19 June.

Kennedy's civil rights bill was music to the ears of those who advocated King's non-violent campaign for change. By 1963 King was regarded by some as "a man who could steer the USA away from racial violence and

Malcolm X addresses a crowd in Harlem, New York, during the early 1960s.

chaos".[4] While Kennedy was no real fan of King, he preferred his brand of civil rights to that espoused by more radical figures such as Malcolm X and the Nation of Islam. Malcolm X was born Malcolm Little in Omaha, Nebraska, in 1925, and became a Muslim while incarcerated for larceny as a young man. Under the tutelage of the Nation of Islam's (NOI) Honourable Elijah Muhammad he developed into a bold, eloquent critic of US racism

and those he regarded as its supporters and lackeys. His prime targets were "Uncle Tom" preachers or "House Negroes", whom he accused of selling out the rest of black America. Prior to his break with the NOI, Malcolm referred to King as "Reverend Chicken Wing". He would also denounce King as a "dreamer" who had failed to wake up to face the nightmare confronting his black brothers and sisters in the USA.

For his part, King cunningly presented Malcolm X as a would-be bogeyman figure for liberal and progressive white Americans; if they wouldn't deal with him, Malcolm X's radical voice was waiting in the wings. Where King's campaigns were black-led but integrated, for most of his public life, Malcolm X ruled out the involvement of white people in the black struggle. He poured scorn on the Council for United Civil Rights Leadership (CUCRL), a white-funded forum established to resolve the inter-organizational wrangles of the SCLC, CORE, NAACP, SNCC, National Council of Negro Women and the Urban League – the so-called "Big Six". As a result, King's SCLC and the other established civil rights groups shunned NOI overtures of black solidarity. Malcolm X and Martin Luther King would briefly meet after a press conference at the US senate on 26 March 1964, spending enough time together to get their picture taken. King would subsequently say of his counterpart, "… he is very articulate, but I totally disagree with many of his political and philosophical views – at least insofar as I understand where he now stands." As the writer Michael Eric Dyson lamented, "[If] King could sit across the table from rabid racists, some of whom sought to murder innocent blacks, and if Malcolm could meet with violent white hate groups to reinforce each other's separatist efforts, then surely they might have discussed their mutual commitment to black freedom."[5]

If Birmingham proved an undoubted success for King, he would scale even greater heights a few months later with the March on Washington (for Jobs and Freedom) on 28 August. The march was the brainchild of A. Philip Randolph, who had first contemplated such a move in 1941 to support the desegregation of US armed forces. Randolph's ideas initially met with resistance from black and white alike. The NAACP's Roy Wilkins was firmly against the involvement of Bayard Rustin as a key organizer, arguing that he should not receive any credit for his involvement. Wilkins, like others, was fearful that Rustin's homosexuality and left-wing sympathies would taint the event. Randolph persuaded King to be part of the march's planning, and the SCLC leader eventually brought on board the NAACP and the Urban League as part of an interracial coalition of religious leaders, workers' groups, and civil rights organizations.

The Kennedy administration was also firmly against the march. At a White House meeting with organizers on 22 June, JFK first took King into the Rose Garden to warn him about the civil rights movement's alleged communist links; he then sought to persuade him that the march was unwise and ill-timed: an act that could undermine his proposed civil rights bill. King retorted that he had "never engaged in a direct-action movement that did not seem ill-timed. Some people thought Birmingham was ill-timed." The president dropped his opposition to the march when it became apparent he could not stop it, but ensured that his administration had such an influence over its orchestration that it was argued that his brother Robert organized it. The involvement of the Kennedy administration and liberal white groups led Malcolm X to denounce the whole event as a farce.

The stated aims of the 28 August rally included "a comprehensive civil rights bill", "protection of the right to vote", "desegregation of all public schools in 1963", and "a Federal Fair Employment Practices Act barring discrimination in all employment". On the day itself, the march proved a magnificent spectacle, involving a quarter of a million to 300,000 people. The huge gathering, which was three-quarters African American and a quarter white and Latino, made its way from the Washington Monument to the Lincoln Memorial, some singing the songs that had become synonymous with the civil rights movement. The day also attracted the great and the good of American show business such as Burt Lancaster, Marlon Brando, Charlton Heston, Sidney Poitier, Harry Belafonte, Sammy Davis Jr, and Lena Horne, and included performers such as Bob Dylan, Joan Baez, Odetta, and Mahalia Jackson. Speeches and vocal contributions were delivered by Walter Reuther, Rabbi Joachim Prinz, Cardinal O'Boyle, Roy Wilkins, Whitney Young, John Lewis, and King himself. Controversy surrounded the initial drafts of Lewis's speech, which reflected the growing disillusionment of the SNCC with the Kennedy administration and the civil rights movement in general. It took the intervention of Bayard Rustin to persuade Lewis to tone down some of his more trenchant comments.

There was no such controversy with King's speech, which proved the highpoint of the march. He arguably spent more time revising and rehearsing that speech than any in his life, only finishing it at 4 a.m. that morning. He knew full well that live television pictures would beam the afternoon's events around the nation, and he did not want to be ill-prepared for the pivotal moment. He did not disappoint. Although his actual speech was short by the standards of his average church sermon, it covered all the salient points of the African-American experience in the USA. In what has become known as his "I Have a Dream" speech, he used language that was rich, powerful, and gushing, and deeply embedded within American history and its psyche. Like all good African-American preachers, he used the timbre of his voice like a master musician to inform, entertain, and excoriate. The speech could be divided into the classic three-act play, with the first section highlighting the failures of the Emancipation Proclamation to deliver real freedom and equality to African Americans. He chose to focus on the indignities and brutalities visited on black people since Lincoln "set them free", and argued that the "promissory note", which guaranteed all Americans the rights of "life, liberty and the pursuit of happiness", had defaulted on African Americans.

The second section introduced the "I Have a Dream" portion, which has since become immortal and was lifted from a sermon King had previously delivered in Detroit, Michigan. At this point, he had found his métier and was firing on all cylinders. The rich, deep voice consistently bellowed out the phrase "I Have a Dream" to highlight his vision for the USA, which at times appeared more in keeping with the book of Revelation than the US Constitution. The last segment revealed the outworkings of his dream for America: faith in a society that truly believes in freedom. This was his new covenant, one that realized Lincoln's promise. His denouement of "Free at last, free at last. Thank God Almighty, we are free at last" was pure black church sermonizing that had the crowd in raptures long after he had left the stage.

Regardless of the criticisms of certain naysayers, the March on Washington was an undoubted success. It also cemented King's status as the USA's premier civil rights leader who was idolized by nearly all African

"I have a dream": A massive crowd gathers on the Mall in the US capital to take part in the March on Washington (for Jobs and Freedom) on 28 August 1963.

Americans and respected by many white people. The Kennedy administration, which had been worried that the march would result in a riot, was pleased with the turn of events. JFK watched the march on television and later invited King and his colleagues to the White House for (non-alcoholic) drinks and talks about the impending civil rights bill.

Barely two weeks after the march, four African-American girls, Denise McNair, Cynthia Wesley, Carole Robertson, and Addie Mae Collins, were killed in the bombing of the prestigious Birmingham Sixteenth Street Baptist Church. The Klansmen killers had planted sticks of dynamite in the church's basement. Once again King returned to the city that only a few months previously had been the scene of his historic victory. This time it was to comfort and calm its African-American residents, and

I HAVE A DREAM

to preach at the children's funerals a few days later. King would spend the rest of his time in the city struggling to contain the black community's fury, and he pondered how "we will keep this [black] fearlessness from rising to violent proportions".

A few days later, JFK summoned King and other leaders to Washington to discuss civil rights. With the Birmingham bombing still fresh in his mind, King told the president: "The Negro community is about reaching breaking point..."[6] JFK's attempts to allay King's fears appeared to mirror his apparent lackadaisical response to the Birmingham bombing, which saw him send the eighty-three-year-old retired General Douglas Macarthur as the White House representative to the girls' funeral. While JFK appeared committed to the passage of the civil rights bill, he showed less commitment to King. At an earlier meeting between the two, King had agreed to sever all links with those civil rights leaders with alleged communist associations. When it came to the president's attention that he had still been in contact with Stanley Levison and Jack O'Dell, a black SCLC organizer who had been a member of the Communist Party, he agreed to J. Edgar Hoover's demands to wiretap King's home phones. One can assume that FBI surveillance was in place at King's home on 22 November 1963 when M. L. heard the news that JFK had been shot while electioneering in Dallas, Texas. Calling Coretta to tell her the news, like most Americans they remained fixed to the television set, awaiting information on their president. When the American people were finally told that their commander-in-chief had succumbed to his bullet wounds, King said to Coretta, "This is what is going to happen to me. I keep telling you, this is a sick society." King would attend John F. Kennedy's funeral in Washington to pay his final respects to a man who, in hindsight, shared many of his foibles. The "King of Camelot" was gone and in his place was the former vice-president, Lyndon Baines Johnson, a man whose Southern Democrat traditions did not appear sympathetic toward either the impending civil rights bill or the concerns of African Americans.

Chapter 6
EYES ON THE PRIZE

The New Year began well for Martin Luther King. Not only was he named *Time* magazine's "Man of the Year" for 1963, he was also summoned to the White House to meet with President Lyndon B. Johnson (LBJ). Alongside the other major civil rights leaders, King expected the new incumbent to adopt a gradualist approach to civil rights. However, President Johnson proved a hard man to assess. Born into virtual poverty in a small Texas town, his family home had no indoor plumbing or electricity. Johnson's biographers suggest that his relative poverty fuelled the ambition of a complex man who was a long-standing member of Congress before becoming the president. His Southern drawl and languid style belied a shrewd mind and manipulative manner, which made him a master at politicking and power games.

LBJ liked to style himself as a reforming president similar to Roosevelt, and it was in this spirit that a short time after getting his six-foot-three-inch-frame behind the Oval Office desk, he met with King and the other civil rights leaders. He impressed upon them his desire to get Kennedy's bill passed "without a word or comma changed". LBJ was true to his word, and by March 1964 the political horse-trading in the senate and then the House of Representatives resulted in what was essentially Kennedy's bill being passed by 289 to 126 votes. It seemed to many in the White House that "there [was] nothing more powerful than an idea whose time ha[d] come". King, along with the leading civil rights leaders, went to Washington to witness President Johnson sign the act on 2 July 1964.

With the ink hardly dry on the act, Johnson gathered together King, Wilkins, Young, and the other leading players, and extolled the virtues

President Lyndon B. Johnson soon
after taking office following John F.
Kennedy's assassination.

of the US legal system which "was securing rights for Negroes". As such,
he regarded any further demonstrations as unnecessary and potentially
counterproductive. Uppermost in his mind was the forthcoming election,
whose outcome was far from certain. LBJ was concerned that his Republican
opponent, the right-wing Arizona senator Barry Goldwater, would opt to
use his support for civil rights as a vote winner. Seeing some logic behind

Black radicals were rapidly losing patience with King's promises, which they claimed delivered little.

Stokely Carmichael (left) and H. Rap Brown (right) take part in an impromptu press conference outside Columbia University's Hamilton Hall, following an African-American occupation of the building to protest against the university's "racist policies".

Johnson's train of thought, King and his colleagues were willing to honour a four-month moratorium on demonstrations. What may have appeared political pragmatism was interpreted as acquiescence by the more radical voices in the SNCC, who moved to distance themselves from this agreement. The developments within the SNCC were symptomatic of the growing militancy among younger African Americans who were seriously critiquing King's non-violent philosophy. Ironically, it was a man who was several years older than King who provided the most trenchant attack on his approach. Malcolm X took King to task about non-violence and the belief that "black people should redeem white people through black bloodshed, sacrifice, and suffering".[1] Although Malcolm X's ideas were undergoing a metamorphosis in 1964, which would include a reassessment of white Americans, he continued to have little time for those who failed to advocate black self-defence in the face of vicious racism.

Malcolm X's words resonated with younger African Americans who were tired of the slow pace of real economic and political change, and the sight of innocent black people being beaten in the struggle to gain the rights enjoyed by white Americans. By 1964, this anger took the form of spontaneous outbreaks of violence in Southern and Northern cities in the USA. According to future SNCC leader and Black Power advocate, Stokely Carmichael, "Each time the black people in those cities saw Dr Martin King get slapped they became angry. When they saw the little black girls bombed to death in a church and civil rights workers ambushed and murdered, they were angrier, and when nothing happened, they were steaming mad." Black radicals were rapidly losing patience with King's promises, which they claimed delivered little. His speeches, which were

invariably peppered with flamboyant metaphors and catchy mantras, were jeered as typical of "De Lawd" – a man enraptured with the cult of personality – promising much yet delivering little. He was denounced as a "sell-out", an African-American flunky in the pay of white benefactors, whose duty it was to mollify black anger in the face of growing white concerns. Indeed, one African-American theologian argued that King's non-threatening message was one of the reasons why white Americans were initially enamoured with him.

King was aware of these criticisms and rebutted accusations that he was a "polished Uncle Tom" traducing his people. He always qualified any criticisms of African Americans who resorted to urban violence by suggesting, "As long as the Negro feels himself on a lonely island in a vast sea of prosperity, there will be the ever-present threat of violence and riots." Words were one thing and actions another, and King's detractors such as James Forman and Stokely Carmichael denounced him as all talk and no action; someone whom they caught eating a steak lunch in his silk pyjamas at his suite in the Gaston Motel, while foot soldiers were in Birmingham's streets demonstrating non-violently. King also made the mistake of failing to consult local New York leaders, such as Adam Clayton Powell, when taking up an invitation from Mayor Robert Wagner to visit the city after uprisings in Harlem and Rochester in July 1964. He was subsequently denounced as a duplicitous interloper more concerned with law and order than attacking the systems and structures which generated the violence. Although King would later criticize the reasons for the uprisings, the media preferred to publicize his measured disapproval of the initial lawlessness.

Civil rights leader and SNCC activist James Forman.

King's struggles to maintain credibility and relevance for his beloved non-violent direct action were only matched by problems at home. His commitment to the civil rights movement meant he spent prolonged periods away from his family, leading to real strains on his relationship with Coretta. By 1964 he was spending as many as three weeks per month away from the marital home, and although he was devoted to his family, his work–life balance meant he was mostly absent during his children's formative years, with telephone calls having to suffice for physical contact. Coretta was left to nurse their children through the usual infant-related illnesses; sing them to sleep at night; supervise play times, and look after their home. Even when he was at home, his day was often consumed with making or receiving telephone calls.

King's marital situation was compounded by his innate chauvinism, which excluded Coretta from civil rights activities. Indeed, SCLC worker Septima Clark suggested: "Dr King didn't think too much of the way women could contribute [to the civil rights movement]." Female commentators would argue that the SCLC office was a testosterone-filled environment that was far from female-friendly. It is said that at times the behaviour and language more resembled a men's social club than a church-related organization, and it can be argued that for King and his colleagues, the civil rights movement was a men's association in all but name.

Another source of tension in the marriage were the whispers of King's philandering. Much is now known of his sexual liaisons as a result of J. Edgar Hoover's covert surveillance of his hotel and motel rooms, and the revelations of his erstwhile friend Ralph Abernathy. King was undoubtedly a ladies' man who satiated his sexual appetite during his college years, and neither time nor marriage restrained his libido. Women of all races found him alluring and, much like a pop star, he was frequently fending off, or succumbing to, the advances of often prim-looking ladies after speaking engagements. Commentators have also suggested that sex appeared to act as both an aphrodisiac and a sedative for King; one that enabled him to assuage the pressures of virtually carrying the civil rights movement (and African-American aspirations) on his squat shoulders. His fixation with sex even found its way into his discourse through his memorable metaphor on segregation as "the adultery of an illicit intercourse between injustice and immorality" that cannot be "cured by the Vaseline of gradualism".

King always believed he had been called by God to lead the civil rights movement. Consequently, he felt answerable to God for his role, which added divine pressures to the already artificial ones. The writer Michael Eric Dyson points out that his behaviour was by no means exceptional for clergymen and something of a concomitant of the veneration they received within certain black communities.[2] Despite this, King was conflicted by his sexual peccadilloes, and experienced bouts of guilt over the way his behaviour contravened Christian teachings, betrayed his marital vows, and questioned his reliability as a civil rights leader.

But there was also a wilful, almost reckless, side to him that appeared to defy good judgment. Even when he became aware of Hoover's surveillance (and the FBI leader's explicit desire to destroy him and the civil rights movement in the process), he failed to curtail his sexual exploits. Many have since contemplated why he would endanger so much for conduct he would denounce from the pulpit as "carnal". In many respects, his reluctance to curb his sexual escapades was curiously reminiscent of his stubborn refusal to completely sever links with supposed communists such as Stanley Levison, Bayard Rustin, and Jack O'Dell. Warned by everyone from JFK to the individuals themselves that such links could destroy him and jeopardize the movement, he remained personal friends with these men, even when he had cut off professional or working ties.

Despite his problems, King pressed on. Conscious that the SCLC was losing ground to the more militant voices in the SNCC, he agreed to turn his attention to the situation developing in St Augustine, Florida. St Augustine, which was established under Spanish rule in 1565, was arguably the USA's oldest city, but one in which terror-driven racism was rife and the effects of the civil rights campaign were nugatory. Dr Robert Hayling, who was head of the St Augustine branch of the NAACP, requested King's services to help in a city where the police and local vigilantes (both with links to the Ku Klux Klan) were virtually indistinguishable. One individual, Holstead "Hoss" Manucy, a bootlegger by trade, marshalled his thugs to carry out all manner of victimization of local African Americans, often with the full knowledge of the sheriff. Previously, Dr Hayling's house had been firebombed, and he and colleagues had also been severely beaten by Klansmen. King dispatched Hosea Williams to St Augustine, where he joined his colleague Dorothy Cotton in her attempts to end segregation, and by March demonstrations and sit-ins began in earnest. The police response, if response is the apt term, was to turn a blind eye to the vigilantes' vicious attacks on demonstrators during their attempts to desegregate beaches, swimming pools, and public facilities. On one occasion, confederate flag-waving lawmen watched on while thugs attacked activists kneeling in prayer at an old slave market.

By the time King arrived in May, the state had elected Haydon Burns, a rampant segregationist, as governor. King would subsequently describe St Augustine as "the most lawless city I've been in, I've never seen this kind of wide open violence". Although he had been warned that his presence was not welcomed, he still came to the city stating his preparedness "to die if ... death is the price I must pay to free my white brother and all my brothers and sisters from a permanent death of the spirit, then nothing can be more redemptive". He immediately set about rallying the troops with powerful speeches at prayer meetings, but found his work stymied by a night marching ban imposed by Sheriff L. O. Davis. King appealed against the injunction, which began on 31 May, and set out on a demonstration on 9 June that ended in his incarceration alongside Ralph Abernathy. Unlike his Birmingham imprisonment, King soon left jail to collect an honorary degree from Yale University. His departure, which had its usual deflationary impact on the movement, coincided with the arrival of sixteen rabbis whose presence only served to add fuel to white vigilante fire. The upsurge in racial violence produced a backlash from sections of the African-American community who were prepared to match fire with fire. Once again, non-violent direct action was under threat and C. T. Vivian was dispatched to black neighbourhoods to control black fury.

King began to worry that St Augustine was turning into another Albany as his attempts to dramatize the situation had failed to generate real impact on either the media or Washington. His call on the federal government to abandon its plans to grant St Augustine $350,000 to mark its quadricentennial in 1965 fell on deaf ears. Likewise, his demands that the governor dispatch state troopers to protect demonstrators and his petitions

to the civic powers to comply with the then civil rights legislation were given short shrift. By the end of June the situation had reached a critical deadlock. At the eleventh hour there appeared an offer of negotiations, which led to the appointment of a biracial committee, and a court order circumscribing the behaviour of law officials. Eager to snatch victory from the jaws of defeat, King hailed these concessions a success, and on the last day of the month beat a hasty face-saving retreat to Atlanta. His supporters would also claim that President Johnson's third and most comprehensive civil rights-related piece of legislation, which was passed a few days later on 2 July, was an outworking of their efforts in St Augustine.

One of the primary reasons for King's eagerness to extricate the SCLC from the virtually intractable situation in St Augustine was the need to focus attention on the Mississippi Freedom Summer activities and the Democratic Convention in the autumn. The Freedom Summer events of 1964, which were also known as "Project Mississippi", were a massive ten-week African-American voter registration scheme in what proved one of the most racially hostile and socially backward states in the USA. Organized by the newly formed Council of Federated Organizations (COFO), consisting of CORE, the NAACP, the SNCC, and the SCLC, the campaign was significant for its deployment of white, Northern civil rights activists. Although white people had always played an active role in the civil rights movement, white participation reached its zenith that summer. Volunteers gathered at a women's college in Oxford, Ohio, in mid June 1964 for orientation and training. The Freedom Summer events were not without their detractors, since some African-American activists were concerned about the dynamics of letting loose groups of educated, assertive but naïve middle-class white

Martin Luther King holds up the photographs of the three young civil rights activists murdered during the 1964 Mississippi Freedom Summer campaign.

Northern students on poor, uneducated African Americans. There were fears that these well-meaning white volunteers would slip into "missionary mode" or fail to submit to local African-American leadership.

Any such campaign in Mississippi was bound to be dangerous, and activists soon found that the involvement of white people only stoked up local white anger in the state. Soon after the project's commencement,

three young activists, Michael Henry Schwerner, Andrew Goodman, and James Chaney were ambushed and murdered in Philadelphia, Mississippi, by Klansmen. The mutilated bodies of Schwerner and Goodman, who were New York Jews, and that of the African-American Mississippian Chaney, were later recovered from a culvert. These brutal murders created a national uproar, forcing interventions from the president and the FBI. Despite federal interest, COFO workers still found themselves subject to mob beatings and harassment, while establishments that supported the campaign, such as churches, were bombed, burned or looted.

Having watched the events from afar, King belatedly joined the campaign at Bob Moses' behest. Moses was the Harlem-born, Harvard educated director of COFO who was primarily tasked with coordinating the Mississippi campaign. Mindful of King's emotional pull on any campaign, he hoped his one-time SCLC colleague would ignite what he knew would be a potentially violent enterprise. Similar to St Augustine, King received his customary death threats from white extremist groups when his involvement became known. He arrived in time to witness the ten-week voters' campaign morph into the emergence of the Mississippi Freedom Democratic Party (MFDP), which claimed to be the most representative Democratic entity in the state. One of the MFDP's prime movers was Fannie Lou Hamer, a forty-seven-year-old matronly African-American civil rights veteran who was known for her blunt, emotionally charged language, delivered in a Mississippi Delta dialect. Although Hamer was from a humble background and unschooled, her accounts of Mississippi racism were spellbinding and persuasive. Her efforts came to the attention of Bob Moses, who drafted her into the movement, and her labours would eventually lead to an

The civil rights activist
Fannie Lou Hamer.

invitation to speak at the (Democratic) Convention's Credentials Committee. Hamer used this opportunity to challenge the state's all-white, anti-civil rights Democratic delegation at the Democratic National Convention (DNC) in Atlantic City, New Jersey. Her stirring televised address not only drew many personal admirers and further support for the MFDP, it also elicited the wrath of President Johnson, who was vexed that her efforts could jeopardize his election chances in the South.

Although King initially supported the MFDP's stance, publicly endorsing its credentials in a statement to the DNC's Credentials Committee, he was subsequently cajoled by the DNC's concession of two at-large seats and a promise to proscribe segregated delegations at the next convention. Hamer's response of "We didn't come all this way for no two seats" echoed the attitude of a growing number of African Americans who were disillusioned with compromises and the belief that real change could not arrive via Washington. This mood coincided with a mounting conviction that white people had little, if any, role to play in the freedom movement.

King was once again forced to navigate his way through the choppy seas of growing black militancy and negotiations with white politicos. He was mindful of the need for black agency within the civil rights movement, and was keen to highlight to the growing number of militants that the SCLC was a black organization (albeit with white advisors and funding). Conversely, he was keen to ensure his campaigns remained interracial and open to the involvement of white folks. At the same time he sought to be a critical friend of white America, and was not afraid to upbraid so-called liberals for their hypocrisy. His *Letter from Birmingham Jail* condemned the duplicity of white liberals, whom he believed were even worse than outright racists. Despite this, many cast him as a dreamer who failed to reflect the growing militancy of African Americans in his conversations with white power structures.

The events of the summer took their toll on King's emotional and physical condition. By 1964, the years of rising before six in the morning and retiring to bed after two the following day began to take their effect. As well as participating in the St Augustine and Mississippi campaigns, King paid visits to Germany and Rome, where he had an audience with Pope Paul VI. The situation was compounded by the SCLC's perilous financial situation, which meant he was forced to undertake extensive fund-raising activities to bolster coffers. When not carrying out these duties, he was supposedly leading the SCLC – a task that became all the more difficult after the protracted departure of Wyatt Tee Walker.

The writer Stewart Burns, whose work on King has explored his emotional state during his public life, describes in detail his depression.[3] Burns points out that his true mental state remained unknown to all but close family and friends, and it was no surprise to them when he was hospitalized at an Atlanta infirmary in mid October to recover from a "virus". His physical and emotional state later brightened in hospital when Coretta told him he had been awarded the Nobel Peace Prize. A clearly excited King said he was "humbly grateful to have been selected for this distinguished honour". He was the youngest recipient at that time and only the second African-American winner.

Records would later show that not everyone was pleased to hear of his accolade. FBI boss J. Edgar Hoover was still smarting over King's criticism of his men during an earlier SCLC-led campaign, and on being told the news of the Nobel prize, he redoubled his efforts to expose King, telling any and everyone that the civil rights leader was a fraud and a danger to national security. Hoover's attempts to expose King to President Johnson singularly failed, as did his efforts at a meeting with a coterie of female journalists to whom he regaled tales of King's sexual behaviour. If Hoover could not destroy King publicly, he sought to do so privately and sent the King household a box containing a barely audible tape recording of his bedroom frolicking. The tape also contained snatches of crude conversations and off-colour jokes involving King. As King was invariably away from home, it was left to Coretta to hear the contents first. A letter, supposedly from an African American but more likely an FBI operative, accompanied the tape, denouncing King as a "fraud" and a "moral delinquent" who ought to kill himself.[4]

This obvious FBI threat forced King into meeting Hoover in early December, where it was hoped some form of truce could be found. The Washington rendezvous was amicable but failed to directly address the reasons why King was in Hoover's office. On leaving the meeting, a smiling King praised Hoover and the FBI for their hard work and dedication, but he was clearly a worried man when he boarded a plane on his way to Oslo to collect his peace prize. He stopped off in London on 6 December for three

Nobel man: Martin Luther King speaks to journalists while Coretta and the children look on. The Kings' large retinue is pictured on its way to Oslo, where King will receive the Nobel Peace Prize.

days of speeches and meetings, the highlight of which was a sermon to a packed St Paul's Cathedral. What was less reported was his meeting with black British activists who equated his struggle with theirs in the UK. King was credited as being the "catalyst" for the emergence of the Campaign Against Racial Discrimination (CARD), the first genuine race-related campaigning organization in Britain.

The King retinue, which included Coretta, his parents, brother A. D., the Abernathys, Bayard Rustin, and other close aides such as Dorothy Cotton, arguably quadrupled the black presence in Scandinavia in 1964. King's mood was still foul; his depression was not helped by news of his brother's late-night sexual shenanigans with Oslo prostitutes at their hotel, or the rambunctious behaviour of the Abernathys. The peace prize ceremony, which took place on 10 December, was a lavish affair in which a well-attired King accepted his award on behalf of the movement and gave a short yet powerful acceptance speech. Although his talk dealt with racial themes, he nonetheless spoke about peace and war, suggesting that he "refused to accept that nation after nation must spiral down a militaristic stairway into the hell of nuclear annihilation". The bestowal of such a prestigious award cemented King's kudos on an international stage and provided the means for his foray into international affairs. His travels in Europe saw him publicly lambaste South Africa for its apartheid, but it was Vietnam, where America was stepping up hostilities to thwart communist influence, that would soon occupy his time and thinking. The ever-munificent King gave the large cheque which accompanied the prize to the SCLC and other civil rights organizations.

The year 1965 saw King drawn into the events taking place in Selma, a town in Dallas County, Alabama, where African-American activists had been fighting, and losing, a near two-year voter registration rights battle. Although African Americans "comprised approximately half of the voting-age population of Dallas County ... [in 1961] only 156 ... out of 15,000 or so, were registered voters".[5] Voting, for black people, had proved virtually impossible due to a prerequisite literacy test that was complicated and served to disenfranchise. The majority of white people were exempt from such tests. Moreover, the bulk of African Americans remained in chronic poverty, with a good many eking out an existence as sharecroppers. Despite interventions from SNCC chairman John Lewis and African-American comedian and activist Dick Gregory, segregation held sway over the newly passed civil rights legislation. Matters went from bad to worse after the Alabama deacon Jimmie Lee Jackson was shot dead by a state trooper during a night-time demonstration on 18 February 1965. The town responded by slapping down a temporary injunction on gatherings discussing civil rights or voter registration.

A now campaign-savvy King was willing to lend support because he knew that in Sheriff James (Jim) Clark he had a perfect adversary for his non-violent strategy. Clark was a burley man cut from the same cloth as Bull Connor – a law officer whose beligerence would effect the dramatization on which King's campaigns depended. King made two visits to Selma in January 1965, the second of which, on 18 January, involved him registering at the all-white Hotel Albert. King's actions caused outrage among certain steadfast segregationists, one of whom attacked the civil rights leader. He faced further rough treatment when Sheriff Clark's men arrested him on 1 February for taking part in a vote-related demonstration.

During King's incarceration (he was released on 5 February), Malcolm X came to town to speak at the Tuskegee Institute. In a meeting with Coretta, he offered words of support, suggesting, "I didn't come to Selma to make his [King's] job more difficult. I really did come thinking that I could make it easier. If the white people realize what the alternative is, perhaps

Sheriff Jim Clark manhandles a female demonstrator during the Selma, Alabama, campaign in 1965.

they will be more willing to hear Dr King." Any further accommodation between the two titans was never forthcoming, as Malcolm X was killed in a hail of bullets in New York on 21 February 1965.

SCLC staffers James Bevel and Diane Nash, who had been active in an Alabama state-wide voting registration campaign, joined SNCC workers to organize a march from Selma to the state capital of Montgomery to petition the segregationist governor George Wallace to protect would-be black registrants. The initial march, which was defying the ban, took place on 7 March 1965 and involved over 500 demonstrators led by the SNCC's John Lewis and the SCLC's Hosea Williams. The march took Highway 80 out of Selma, and after a relatively quiet start, the situation turned ugly when the demonstrators confronted Colonel Al Lingo's state troopers and Sheriff Clark's lawmen on the Edmund Pettus Bridge. When the demonstrators failed to accede to troopers' orders to disperse and return home, instructions were given to disband the crowd. The events that day became known as "Bloody Sunday" because of the orgy of violence meted out by the lawmen on demonstrators. The SNCC's John Lewis was beaten senseless, and only the more fortunate demonstrators left the bridge unbloodied, as the lawmen liberally deployed clubs, fists, and tear gas. This entire melee was captured by television cameras, which broadcast the violence to a horrified nation and a vexed White House.

One such onlooker was King, who immediately garnered a cross section of support for a further march he intended to lead a few days later. Against the advice of the president, King led a 2,500-member throng toward the Edmund Pettus Bridge and the route to Montgomery, in apparent defiance of the earlier injunction. What followed baffled some and angered others, as King halted the march on the bridge, led demonstrators in prayer and singing, and then gave instructions for the marchers to return to Selma. Thus, King had not technically defied the injunction, and had avoided the potential violence of state troopers. However, the "Tuesday Turnaround", as it was dubbed, angered the more militant demonstrators, who accused him of everything from compliance to cowardice. Later that evening, Selma Klansmen attacked the recently arrived white Bostonian clergyman, James J. Reeb, leaving him for dead. Reeb's death a few days later caused a further national outcry and resulted in a meeting between the president and Governor George Wallace. (There was a similar outcry over the Klan-related killing of Viola Gregg Liuzzo, a white Detroit housewife in Lowndes County, leading some SNCC supporters to juxtapose the response to these white killings with that of Jimmie Lee Jackson.)

All these deaths and the mayhem in Selma saw a stern-looking President Johnson address Congress in a televised session in which he argued, "Their cause must be our cause too. Because it is not just Negroes, but really it is all of us, who must overcome the crippling legacy of bigotry and injustice. And we shall overcome." Johnson's words proved a salve to civil rights activists, especially King, who apparently cried on hearing the president use his language during his monumental speech. On 17 March, Johnson submitted voting rights legislation to Congress. A judicial ruling to overturn the marching injunction followed his bill, and on 21 March, King led a multiracial march of over 8,000 demonstrators, including the entertainers Nina Simone and Harry Belafonte (accompanied by National Guardsmen), toward Montgomery. By the time the bandwagon rolled into Montgomery on 25 March, numbers had swelled to 25,000. Perching

Civil rights marchers gather on the Edmund Pettus Bridge during the Selma to Montgomery protest in 1965.

on the steps of the State Capitol Building, King delivered his stirring "How Long, Not Long" speech to an enthusiastic Montgomery crowd. The previous week's events had not diminished his capacity to induce hope, and his speech used biblical saints and modern-day civil rights martyrs such as Medgar Evers, Jimmie Lee Jackson, and Reverend James Reeb as an inspiration for a righteous battle he believed would end in victory. Coming almost a decade after his first foray into civil rights, and in the very same state, King hailed the march and campaign a success. It led to improved voter registration and the desegregation of public accommodations. Indeed, civil rights activists, especially those in the SCLC, would later suggest that Selma proved a catalyst for the Voting Rights Act which came into effect on 6 August 1965.

Chapter 7
KEEP ON KEEPING ON

The Selma campaign asked as many questions as it answered about the state of the civil rights movement in the mid sixties, as it highlighted the differences between the SCLC and the SNCC over tactics and the ethnic composition of campaigns. The SNCC's increasing militancy sought to minimize white involvement and increase greater grass roots participation in voter registration. Many SNCC supporters criticized Selma as a "media-centred march", arguing that the large numbers of demonstrators should have been used for a door-to-door mass voter registration campaign. One cultural critic writing at the time suggested that "the Selma campaign had cemented the notion, in the minds of the more honest civil rights campaigners, that the movement had reached a strategic impasse, which revolved around them being able to utilise demonstrations to dramatise injustice and get laws passed, but lacked the power and wherewithal to ensure those laws were enforced".[1] The crux of this argument was that no sooner did the SCLC bandwagon leave town than the authorities reneged on promises to desegregate public facilities or hire the commensurate number of African-American staff. Such a scenario usually required King to return several times to the scene of his "victory" to ensure agreements were upheld. A good case in point was the Birmingham campaign, where he was forced to revisit the city on a number of occasions to ensure it made good on its agreed deal.

Once again, external problems mirrored those within the SCLC. Staff morale, which had never been great, was reaching near rock bottom. As one would expect with an establishment full of capable, ambitious men, there were tensions. Arguments broke out over who would succeed King if the unthinkable occurred. After his umpteenth death threat during the Selma campaign, King had agreed to install Ralph Abernathy as his successor. In many people's eyes, Abernathy's increasing ambition never matched his ability, and he was largely seen as an amiable bumbling Dr Watson-style foil to the brilliant (but flawed) Sherlock Holmes-like King. Many, including Daddy King, were upset with this choice, and thought the top job should go to someone such as Andrew Young, who appeared to have everything that Abernathy lacked.

The writer David Garrow has also documented the many squabbles within the SCLC, particularly over leadership roles and power. The often-heated relationship between James Bevel and Wyatt Tee Walker was only resolved by the departure of the latter. Arguments then ensued over who would replace Walker. There was also perpetual jockeying for greater support for certain initiatives. James Bevel and Hosea Williams clashed over the latter's Summer Community Organization and Political Education (SCOPE) voter registration project in the Deep South. For Bevel and Randy Blackwell, Walker's replacement, SCOPE was an expensive exercise in ego massaging that the SCLC could ill afford. In the words of one writer. SCOPE became "an experiment in liquor and sex, compounded by criminal conduct".[2] Bevel wanted to build on the gains of Selma and urged the SCLC to take part in a mass civil disobedience campaign across Alabama to bring down its tyrannical governor, George Wallace. When not calling for the non-violent kidnapping of Governor Wallace, Bevel and his then wife, Diane Nash, were coaxing the SCLC to turn its attention northward. since in their minds the passing of civil rights laws had seen the defeat of state-sponsored segregation in the South. When the SCLC failed to fully back their scheme, the Bevels took matters into their own hands and moved to Chicago in late 1965.

While many may not have shared Bevel's sanguine analysis of the South, there was little doubt that an equally pernicious and entrenched form of racism existed in the North, with big cities such as Boston, Detroit, Cleveland, Philadelphia, and Chicago containing so-called ghettoes. For many African Americans, the North had been the place to which their former enslaved forebears had fled to escape servitude. The writer James Gregory points out that black newspapers in the South were at the forefront of the propaganda encouraging the exodus from the South, and were replete with stories of work opportunities in Northern industries. African Americans had moved out of the South in the 1940s, taking up employment occasioned by the Second World War and the munitions industries. This served to solidify the burgeoning black community, and changed the demographics of cities such as Chicago, New York, Detroit, and Los Angeles. As African Americans moved in, white people moved out as part of the "White Flight" to the suburbs.

All the talk of "milk and honey" in the North proved fallacious for most African Americans, who found themselves living in the poorest, most rundown sections of cities. With high rents and even higher crime rates, many exchanged rural poverty for a rat-infested urban equivalent. Gainful employment was similarly difficult, with most struggling to obtain the same jobs and wages as their white counterparts. Equally, educational opportunities were nugatory and many students struggled in overcrowded, poorly equipped schools. One black commentator argued that while Southern civil rights activists were fighting to eradicate separate drinking fountains, Northern inner city black people were fighting to *obtain* drinking fountains.

The SCLC was bounced into action in the North through the massive insurrection in Watts, a largely black district in Los Angeles known for its paucity of decent local amenities and over-zealous policing. The disturbances, which began on 11 August 1965, were ignited by the arrest of an alleged drunk driver and his passengers, but inflamed by years of dysfunctional law enforcement. After the six days of unrest had subsided in the City of Angels, thirty-four people had lost their lives, a further 1,000 were injured, and almost 3,500 had been arrested. Unlike in Rochester, New York, the previous year, King did not play the "law and order" card, but

Black and white people drink from separate water fountains in the Deep South.

during his visit a few days later, he tempered any censure with a withering critique of the social causes that led to the violence. And to paraphrase Victor Hugo, he acknowledged that violence was often the language of the unheard. His admission revealed the unacknowledged truth that several days' violence could make more of a visceral impact than a thousand peaceful marches. He was also aware that for some African Americans "rocks, boulders and incendiary devices were a cathartic way of giving white folks a taste of their own violent medicine". The one-time SNCC firebrand, (Hubert) H. Rap Brown, would take the point further and argue that America would always take heed of anything violent since "violence [was] as American as cherry pie" – a way of life since *The Mayflower*. While King may have understood these sentiments, he believed that burning down one's neighbourhood only exacerbated the already hellish conditions.

The events that August clearly demonstrated the anger and despair of African Americans in Northern cities; Watts was "one of the first of 239 outbreaks of racial violence in over 200 US cities in the 'five hot summers' of 1964–1968. Almost every American city outside of the South was at some stage affected..."[3] Aware that his organization was perceived as being Southern in both name and focus, and that its campaigns had failed to have a tangible impact on African Americans living in the North, the prophet of hope sought to bring his dream to its nightmarish cities. The real debate was whether King's particular brand of non-violent tactics, which was fashioned in Southern fires, could function in Northern furnaces. Moreover, by taking his campaign to the North, the SCLC would become a de facto national organization, putting it on a par (and in competition) with the NAACP and other national civil rights groups.

After much discussion. it was agreed to focus on Chicago, which was home to over a million African Americans, many of whom had fled to the Windy City's South and West sides after migrating from the Deep South a generation earlier. Chicago was deemed the "Birmingham of the North", not only in the way the unwritten laws and social mores kept the large black population in its place, but also in the belief that if this dam could be breached, it would release the floodgates across the North.

King was initially invited to the city in July 1965 to take part in what was ostensibly a schools and housing rally organized by civil rights activist and teacher Albert Raby, who convened the Coordinating Council of Community Organizations (CCCO).

At the start of 1966, he joined James Bevel and an SCLC advanced guard who had been scoping the city since the previous autumn. Aware of Chicago's racial problems, King was keen to mobilize an ethnically inclusive coalition to fight for better housing, jobs, and an enhancement of local amenities to improve the quality of life. In an attempt to be "incarnational", he moved his family into one of the infamous slum apartments in Lawndale, in the city's West Side. However, prior to collecting the keys, the decorators carried out home improvements, ensuring that his experiences were far from authentic. Despite this, the sheer oppressive nature of inner city living, with its concrete jungles, dearth of public spaces, and grinding poverty, soon affected the behaviour of his children. King would spend most of the week in Chicago and return to Atlanta at the weekend to carry out his duties at Ebenezer.

Meanwhile, Bevel worked with locals to establish neighbourhood tenant unions to fight slum landlords with their extortionate rents. And

Martin Luther King is
restrained while taking
part in a demonstration.

what became the Chicago Freedom Movement launched a campaign for banks to offer more loans and mortgages, and real estate agents to widen the number of properties to break down the tacit segregation in the city. Such a campaign meant crossing swords with Richard J. Daley, the Irish-Catholic mayor who ran the city with an iron fist thanks to patronage (including the collusion of black leaders), close links to the Democratic Party, and alleged mob connections. The wily mayor sought to wrong-foot or parry King at every juncture, initially claiming to share his vision for improved housing, and making cosmetic renovations to some of the worst slum properties. Daley later held a press conference to talk up his own dream for Chicago,

while criticizing King's lack of vision. King dismissed Daley for "playing games", but despite the demonstrations and marches (King was felled by a rock on one march) the campaign was soon floundering.

Once again it appeared that without a Bull Connor or Jim Clark-like figure it was difficult to dramatize the campaign's efforts. Moreover, despite the de facto ethnic divide in the city, there were no "whites only" lunch counters or drinking fountains which contravened

Chicago, the city that witnessed the SCLC's first Northern campaign.

the new civil rights legislation, and King struggled to make the moral case for his efforts in Chicago. While many Northern white Americans were content to see the dark deeds of their Southern white counterparts exposed, they were unhappy to have the race spotlight shone on them. More importantly, they simply refused to equate the conditions of African Americans in the North with those in the South. As a result, King's campaign in the North was deemed unnecessary and an act of pure hubris.

The shooting of the civil rights activist James Meredith on 6 June 1966 interrupted King's faltering Chicago campaign. Meredith, who had helped to desegregate the University of Mississippi in 1962, had decided – some would argue unwisely – to organize a well-publicized solo 220-mile March Against Fear from Memphis, Tennessee, to Jackson, Mississippi. Meredith was shot by a racist sniper a few days into his march, and on hearing the news King flew to his hospital bed, where he vowed to finish the march. He was joined by Floyd McKissick, the new head of CORE, and Stokely Carmichael, who had replaced John Lewis as the SNCC's new chair. Carmichael was a lean, angular-featured, Trinidad-born, New York-raised firebrand who by 1966 had real issues with King. His reference points were rooted in Malcolm X's fury prior to his break with the Nation of Islam, and he never appeared to buy into the non-violence philosophy. After wrestling the SNCC leadership from John Lewis, Carmichael continued the organization's radicalism. He found a perfect ally in CORE's Floyd McKissick, a man who was also keen to deviate from non-violence as both a tactic and a philosophy.

The Meredith march, which was always going to be difficult under the circumstances, was not helped by the attendance of white state troopers who appeared more interested in harassing demonstrators than maintaining law and order. Equally, Byron De La Beckwith, who was later convicted of killing Medgar Evers, hurled racist abuse from a pick-up that drove up and down the highway during the long march. It therefore came as no surprise that on the first day of the march, an altercation took place between Carmichael and a trooper which ended with King non-violently restraining the SNCC leader. Although King and Carmichael insisted on marching arm-in-arm they were poles apart, and the media began to sense both the tensions and divisions. The fissures were torn open that evening when at a meeting in James Lawson's church in Memphis, Carmichael suggested that black people seize power in the areas of the South where

*White state
troopers ... appeared
more interested
in harassing
demonstrators than
maintaining law
and order.*

they formed a majority. As for himself, he argued that he was not going to beg the white man for anything; he was going to take it!

King moved to qualify and distance himself from the more inflammatory aspects of Carmichael's speech, but he was soon forced to use all of his persuasive skills to ensure the march remained integrated and non-violent, after Carmichael had questioned white involvement, and argued that the Deacons for Defense and Justice, an African-American paramilitary-style group who often brandished firearms, join as bodyguards. The already tense march continued, with a greater edge provided by some SNCC marchers singing, "Jingle bells, shotgun shells, freedom all the way. Oh what fun it is to blast a trooperman away." By the time the marchers reached Greenwood on 16 June, Carmichael was in no mood for compromise, and at a meeting that evening he called for black people to take matters into their own hands and demand "Black Power". According to Carmichael, "Black Power advocates were quite clear in [their] own minds that a 'non violent' approach to civil rights [was] an approach black people [could] not afford and a luxury white people [did] not deserve."[4] King was quick to caution against the usage of the term and quell any media confusion. He attacked Black Power as an ideology that was both unattainable and self-defeating in a society constructed around white hegemony. He was also concerned about its tacit links between power and violence, and believed that it was not the strategy to effect real black liberation.

But his leadership of the march seemed in jeopardy. The SNCC marchers preferred to talk among themselves while King spoke at meetings; they had moved from jeering to indifference. The more revolutionary-minded

Martin and Malcolm: the first and only recorded meeting between Martin Luther King and Malcolm X occurred in Washington in 1964.

supporters were suggesting that time had caught up with King. At this juncture, the more militant African Americans were using the word "black" instead of "Negro", which was more in keeping with the growing black consciousness/pride movement in the USA. While no Black Power advocate, King did embrace black pride, having long called for "black somebodiness", which he equated with his notion of black people being "made in the image of God". King would elucidate these ideas in the last book he wrote, *Where Do We Go from Here: Chaos or Community?*,[5] a powerful treatise which clearly demonstrated that he was in touch with the zeitgeist of black political thought. Despite this, his placid persona, bombastic language, and preference to still use the term "Negro", coupled with his conservative dress and solid church background, left him open to accusations of being an "Uncle Tom". He was undoubtedly angered by such condemnation and would argue that he was prepared to "put his life on the line for his people" in terrifying towns and cities such as Albany, Birmingham, St Augustine, and Selma; something which some of his more vocal detractors, such as Malcolm X, had failed to do.

While he publicly denounced Black Power he was undoubtedly influenced by it, and his language and attitude became sharper after the Meredith march and his experiences in Chicago. He would propose that "White America never did intend to integrate housing, integrate schools or be fair with the Negro about jobs". And according to one writer he told black audiences that "... the vast majority of white Americans are racists".[6]

The notion of a beloved community also appeared a cruel hallucination in Chicago, whose ethnic neighbourhoods were little more than a ruse to disenfranchise African Americans. Undeterred, King stepped up his campaign in the city after the Meredith hiatus, determined that his demonstrations would extract concessions from the stubborn Daley. On 10 July he led a march to City Hall where, in the style of his German Protestant namesake, he sought to pin a list of demands to the building's doors. There was unrest later in a black neighbourhood over heavy-handed police attempts to shut off a fire hydrant. King's efforts to becalm the situation were dismissed by Daley, who blamed his presence for the riot. He was also attacked by black Chicagoans such as the Vice Lords gang, who suggested he had failed to address their grievances. Once again, King stared defeat in the face.

Desperate times called for desperate measures, and in what could only be described as an act of desperation, Jesse L. Jackson, an SCLC activist who headed up Operation Breadbasket, the job integration programme, proposed a march in the hostile white neighbourhood of Cicero. Even at the best of times, a black face was persona non grata in Cicero – a march consisting of a plethora of black faces would be an incendiary act. It is a credit to King's courage that he declared he would not only march to Cicero, but set up camp if need be. Just the sheer thought of the carnage and the resulting news footage forced the intransigent Daley to meet with King and arrive at an accommodation.

The scheming mayor ensured that the agreement secured on ending housing discrimination amounted to little. While King agreed to halt his marches with immediate effect, no timetable was placed on housing agreements, which were little more than good intentions. However, at a prima facie level, King could claim to have exacted concessions from Daley, and he wasted no time claiming to have snatched another victory from the

A young Jesse Jackson addresses a crowd during an Operation Breadbasket rally.

jaws of defeat. The writer Taylor Branch quotes those who regarded the campaign as a failure from beginning to end, accusing King of being "long on eloquence, but short on concrete objectives".[7] It was also argued that the SCLC campaign in Chicago lacked both strategy and tactical nous: marches were carried out at weekends rather than weekdays, when city centre demonstrations would have paralysed businesses and the administration of government. King's exploits in the North (Chicago) and the South (Mississippi March against Fear) in 1966 further weakened his unofficial headship of the civil rights movement. His charisma had its limitations against devious white politicos on the one hand and radical, belligerent black voices on the other.

Moreover, unlike the NAACP and National Urban League, King's failure to fully criticize Black Power militants resulted in a haemorrhaging of white supporters who were frightened by the growing militancy within the civil rights movement. Conversely, would-be black supporters became attracted to the no-nonsense, hyper masculine approach of groups such as the emergent Black Panthers, whose talk of "pigs" (the police), Franz Fanon, Chairman Mao's *Little Red Book*, and self-defence proved affirming and empowering. What further exacerbated the situation was the media's fixation with these new, radical groups. King could only watch on as the US media gave the full oxygen of publicity to the often wild and inflammatory remarks of Eldridge Cleaver, Huey P. Newton, H. Rap Brown, and Bobby Seale, as much to embarrass King as to stir up fear-driven responses from white Americans. These "Burn, Baby, Burn" protestations played upon latent white fears that black people were seeking to exact retribution on white society for slavery and racism.

> *Would-be black supporters became attracted to the no-nonsense, hyper masculine approach of groups such as the emergent Black Panthers.*

King was also aware that many white Americans had become disillusioned with the whole civil rights agenda, believing African Americans were either obtaining the lion's share of the federal funds emerging from the "war on poverty", which formed part of LBJ's Great Society programme, or ungrateful. They cited Daniel Patrick Moynihan's much-trumpeted "The Negro Family: The Case For National Action" report,[8] which referred to affirmative action to alleviate the problems of African Americans. When the findings were denounced as patronizing by certain African Americans, some white people argued that they were unappreciative of state support and "did not know when to stop". Indeed, some white Americans told Johnson the situation had gone far enough in favour of African Americans, and that they were frightened of the "dangers to the national well-being ... from another round of urban riots".[9]

By late 1966, Johnson's energies were more consumed with the US's engagement in Vietnam than civil rights, and it has been suggested the only "race" he was concerned with was prefixed either by "arms" or "space". As commander-in-chief, Johnson oversaw Operation Rolling Thunder, the mass aerial bombardment of North Vietnam which began in the spring of 1965, and ended with his presidency. These bombings coincided with massive troop increases from 5,000 during his first year in office to 100,000 by March 1965. The numbers continued to grow exponentially, reaching 500,000 by the end of 1967. As troop numbers grew, so did fatalities. King took a keen interest in the Vietnam War, juxtaposing war-related expenditure overseas with the demands for economic (and social) justice for all citizens in the USA. He condemned the fact that over 35 million Americans lived in poverty while the country squandered millions on an overseas war.

King had turned his attention to Vietnam as early as 1965, and at the SCLC convention in August that year he called for a cessation of the bombing of North Vietnam. He also urged diplomatic negotiations involving the United Nations to prevent further conflict in the region. However, at this moment in time, he was wary of going any further for fear of upsetting President Johnson, who was deemed sympathetic toward the civil rights issue. Equally, King was worried about being labelled a communist. Despite this, he believed his role as a Christian preacher forced him to speak out against the war, and later that year he described the conflict, like all war, as an evil that must be opposed. He finally decided to up the anti-war ante while on holiday in Ocho Rios, Jamaica, in January 1967. He was meant to be relaxing and drafting what would be *Where Do We Go from Here?* when his tranquillity was disturbed after picking up an issue of *Ramparts*, the left-wing political and literary magazine, which included a searing account of the war in Vietnam. The contents caused the normally food-hungry King to lose his appetite, and he told his personal assistant, Bernard Lee, that he would not eat well again until he did something about the war, regardless of the consequences.

He condemned the fact that over 35 million Americans lived in poverty while the country squandered millions on an overseas war.

King knew the costs of high-profile African-American opposition to the war: Muhammad Ali, the undisputed world heavyweight boxing champion, was being hauled before the courts for refusing the Vietnam War draft. Ali was questioning the duplicity of sending disproportionate numbers of African Americans half way around the world to fight for freedoms they were denied at home. In spite of this, many within the civil rights movement were opposed to King's stance on Vietnam and thought it both unwise and poor timing to conflate the two issues. The NAACP and National Urban League, always the most conservative of the civil rights organizations, warned King that his diversion into international politics could make a potential enemy out of the US president. There were even rumbles within the SCLC, with the normally radical Bayard Rustin advising against such a stance. In order to placate his colleagues, King initially agreed to speak on these issues as a pastor rather than SCLC leader. On Capitol Hill he was denounced as arrogant and naïve – a man whose delusions of grandeur had led to him overreaching himself. His credentials to speak on foreign policy and matters of war and peace were questioned, despite him being a Nobel Peace Prize winner. He was also accused of naked opportunism and ambition, and it was argued that he had segued into Vietnam because he had taken the civil rights movement as far as it could go.

Fresh from his Jamaican break, King used every opportunity to speak out against the Vietnam War. His stance placed him alongside figures embracing the counterculture, such as hippies, students, and the political left in the USA. He joined the likes of Dr Spock, the famous paediatrician and anti-war campaigner, whom Coretta had shared a stage with a few years

earlier at a Washington rally. King delivered two damning denunciations in Chicago and Los Angeles, critiquing the USA as an agent of war rather than peace and conflict resolution. His sermons at his native Ebenezer were also platforms for honing his anti-war rhetoric.

King would deliver his most stinging attack at the historic Riverside Church in New York on 4 April 1967 where in front of a packed congregation, which included Rabbi Abraham Joshua Heschel and Amherst College professor Henry Commagerat, he explained why he was speaking out against the war. After he had responded to his detractors, he launched into excoriating his country for its arrogance and belligerence. In his mind, the USA's wealth and power had led to an imperial-like attitude to world affairs, making it "the greatest purveyor of violence in the world today". His carefully crafted and forcefully delivered "Beyond Vietnam" speech also contained a five-point plan for ending the war and improving the US's standing on the world stage.

For all its expressive eloquence and cogent arguments, King's detractors saw his "Beyond Vietnam" speech as a clear sign that he had lost the plot, and *Time* magazine, which only three years previously had named him "Man of the Year", denounced it as "demagogic slander that sounded like a script for Radio Hanoi". A *Washington Post* editorial went even further, suggesting King had "diminished his usefulness to his cause, his country and his people". Criticism also came from supposed friends such as the African-American scholar and fellow Nobel Prize winner Ralph Bunche, who attacked King's fusion of local and international issues, and pleaded that he choose one or the other. Worse was to follow. At a New York City reception, King encountered the Urban League's Whitney Young, who

World heavyweight boxing
champion Muhammad Ali.

*King openly declared
his opposition to the
Vietnam War.*

had publicly criticized him on Vietnam. King upbraided Young for his comments, implying that he was more concerned about holding on to foundation grants from conservative organizations than doing the right thing. An aggrieved Young pointed to King's girth protruding from his well-cut suit and flashed back, "You're eating well!" The normally calm King had to be pulled away from Young.

While these criticisms did not thwart King's stance on Vietnam, they took a toll on his health. His legendary love of soul food (a selection of traditional African-American cuisine) became comfort eating, and photographs of him toward the end of his life reveal significant weight gain. He also upped his nicotine intake but still ensured he kept his habit from the public glare. A further form of refuge was found in the whisky bottles to which he regularly turned on those nights in motels and hotels after speaking engagements. Moreover, his various pronouncements on civil rights and the state of the USA became bleaker, leading some to believe that the "prophet of hope" was losing his. Colleagues such as Dorothy Cotton, the long-term SCLC staffer, would later recount how he spoke about feeling "tired" from all the burdens of leadership, and lamented: "The Lord called [me] to be a preacher, and not to do all this stuff...' For Cotton, King's anti-war stance only heaped further pressures on him.

After King openly declared his opposition to the Vietnam War, he became the darling of the anti-war movement, in demand by them as a speaker and spokesperson. He provided a voice for many white students and recent graduates who were now at an age to be drafted into a war that was killing and maiming Americans in their thousands. Although Robert Kennedy, the bright and ambitious brother of the late JFK, would subsequently be one of

Whitney Young, executive director of the National Urban League.

the few leading Democratic politicians to attack US policy in Vietnam, in the spring of 1967 it was left to the likes of King to take up the political mantle of anti-war agitator. This led some within the peace movement to ask King to stand in the forthcoming presidential elections. King resisted all calls to enter the political fray, believing he could best serve the cause as an outsider, free from the political wheeler-dealing of Washington. However, his politics had polarized supporters, especially those with the gift of giving, leading to a shortfall in financial donations to the SCLC. Indeed, the SCLC's plummeting finances echoed King's standing across the nation; by the end of 1967 there was little chance of him winning any "Man of the Year" award in the USA.

King regarded the Vietnam War as part of a malaise affecting his country, and one which could only be cured by a radical change to society. As a student he had studied Marx, and he was privately fascinated by his "great passion for social justice, but [believed he] had fallen afoul of the theoretical errors of materialism". And while not arguing for American-style communism, King urged the USA to abandon capitalism in favour of democratic socialism. (He preferred to keep his more radical political ideas to himself for fear of being labelled a communist.) At this juncture he realized that his belief in the human capacity to change could not transform America into a bastion of freedom and equality. The legislative gains made in previous years, while good on paper, had made tangibly few changes to the black community. Most were still poor and disenfranchised. King had begun to argue that nothing short of a Marshall Plan would resolve these myriad woes. Yet he was acutely aware that poverty transcended racial lines and was very much a class-bound issue, revolving around the haves and the have-nots. At an SCLC retreat in Frogmore, South Carolina, in November 1966, he argued, "There is something wrong with the economic system of our nation ... something is wrong with capitalism." He suggested that capitalism was incapable of delivering real justice and equality since it was by its very nature abusive and divisive, and formed the basis of the "triple evils" of racism, economic exploitation, and militarism. It was this thinking that led him to contemplate leading a Poor People's Campaign (PPC) in Washington DC in spring 1968. The PPC would prove his most ambitious campaign to date, and one which set him on a direct collision course with big business and those in Washington.

Chapter 8
I MAY NOT GET THERE WITH YOU

W hile King took most of the credit for the PPC, which planned to dramatize economic issues, it was the brainchild of African-American lawyer Marian Wright, who had been on the NAACP's legal defence team. The April demonstration involved the establishment of a large camp which in true Gandhi style would paralyse the administration and day-to-day life of Washington DC. Such a high stakes venture would be personally and professionally dangerous, and King warned participants that they should expect to be incarcerated. One writer has suggested that King may have regarded a stretch in prison as "the only possible refuge ... from the ordeal his mission had become".[1]

Like all King's campaigns, the PPC was attacked as ill-conceived and emblematic of his descent into political extremism. What made the criticism distinctive was the direction from which it came, with many SCLC stalwarts totally against the campaign. With the exception of Andrew Young, mainstays such as James Bevel believed it was a distraction from Vietnam, while the increasingly significant Jesse Jackson thought more effort should be given to his Operation Breadbasket programme. The internal disaffection was indicative of the lack of clear leadership within the SCLC, which was exacerbated by the departure of personnel such as Bayard Rustin. Those brought in to provide vision and structure, such as William Rutherford, were either ignored or sidelined by hubristic SCLC workers.

In an attempt to secure supporters for his campaign, King set off on a recruitment drive in the Deep South. He increasingly believed that the PPC was a final throw of the dice to avoid racial Armageddon and create his beloved community. He sought to develop alliances between poor blacks, whites, and Latinos, who were victims of the same exploitative capitalist system. Nonetheless his attempts to recruit supporters for the PPC were far from successful in the South, where centuries of racism and suspicion could not be overcome by his persuasive words and the promise of a convivial break in Washington.

According to one writer, his attempts among black people also failed because of the FBI's subversion tactics. In January 1968 "Hoover had instructed 22 field officers to coordinate intelligence gathering on the PPC with local and state police".[2] And its Ghetto Information Program "utilized over 3,000 ghetto residents as 'listening posts'. They were paid to report on and thwart SCLC recruitment efforts for the PPC." It was made known that any PPC participants "would have their welfare benefits cut off". These clandestine programmes were part of the FBI's Counter Intelligence Program (or COINTELPRO), which had existed since 1956 to undermine "unAmerican activities" such as communism. On 25 August 1967 it launched activities against "black Hate Groups",[3] focusing on the Nation of Islam, SCLC, CORE, and SNCC. Conversely, some white people were fearful that the campaign could descend into the type of racial violence overtaking many US cities, while others equated the poverty campaign as a back door crusade to expand welfare provision and other forms of state-based reliance.

The PPC's efforts fared better in the North, where coordinator Bernard Lafayette recruited more conscientious community and religious groups in Washington DC and Philadelphia. King received a fillip in the form of Otto Kerner's exhaustive report of February 1968 into the recent civil disorders in US cities, which concluded that the country was becoming more racially polarized. Its solution involved the implementation of extensive (and

> *"We can stick together. You are demonstrating that we are all tied in a single garment of destiny, and that if one black person suffers, if one black person is down, we are all down."*

expensive) programmes to right historic wrongs against African Americans. Congressman Kerner's remedy appeared to chime with King's call for the availability of $30 billion of federal funds to alleviate poverty. Yet the report did not stop King from worrying whether he could recruit the necessary 2,000 demonstrators for the campaign, and he considered postponing or even cancelling the event. However, his struggle to gain recruits was overtaken by a call from James Lawson, who had become embroiled in the African-American sanitation workers' campaign for better pay and conditions in Memphis. This labour crusade had become crystallized after the work-related deaths of two black workers, Echol Cole and Robert Walker, on 1 February 1968, which had led to a mass walkout. Efforts to join the American Federation of State, County, and Municipal Employees (AFSCME) union brought the workers into contact with the NAACP, which agreed to support a strike on 11 February 1968.

By the time Lawson placed a call to King, other civil rights leaders such as Bayard Rustin were involved in taking up the case of the sanitation workers. Lawson subsequently formed Community on the Move for Equality (COME), which aimed to exact reforms from the newly elected Mayor Henry Loeb, a power-obsessed autocrat whose intransigence was reminiscent of Governor George Wallace. COME also aimed to secure the support of the city's African-American middle classes and the black church, both of which appeared to snub the sanitation workers, perhaps because of their apparent lowly status. King had no such qualms, seeing them as exemplary of the PPC – many were forced to supplement their meagre earnings with food stamps. King's initial decision to join Lawson in Memphis was queried by Andrew Young, who believed the campaign would be an unwelcome distraction

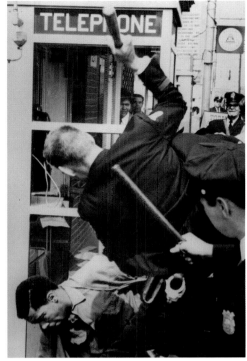

Police club an African-American demonstrator during the riots that broke out after the Martin Luther King-led Memphis march.

from his Washington efforts. King parried these concerns by stating that it was his responsibility to stand with the poor, wherever they lived.

At a packed indoor meeting in Memphis on 18 March, King commended the strikers for showing that "... we can stick together. You are demonstrating that we are all tied in a single garment of destiny, and that if one black person suffers, if one black person is down, we are all down." His powerful invocation was very much the stimulus the black community needed. The burgeoning strike faced fierce resistance from Mayor Loeb, who had no qualms about allowing police to use tear gas and mace to break up one non-violent march to City Hall. King's involvement also garnered the backing of many of the city's white students, who offered vociferous support for what became daily protests in the city.

As with all SCLC associated campaigns, King called for a showpiece event to dramatize the protest. Pre-empting aspects of his PPC strategy for Washington, he suggested a citywide work stoppage on 22 March as part of a mass protest that he would lead. As the campaign was not an SCLC orchestrated one, he was reliant on James Lawson and his COME colleagues to ensure events went to plan. Initially the weather conspired against King, as an unseasonal snowstorm caused the last minute curtailment of the demonstration. Unperturbed by this turn of events, it was agreed to rearrange the demonstration for 28 March. This new date

Las Brisas, Acapulco Bay, Mexico.

proved the climatic opposite, and was hot and balmy. Events began badly with the late arrival of King due to plane problems. By the time he and Abernathy made their way through lines of demonstrators brandishing placards bearing the words "I AM A MAN" to lead the march, the two-hour delay had caused an already agitated crowd to be primed for action. Unbeknown to King, the crowd included members of the Invaders, a Memphis-based Black Power group, with little time for non-violence and integrated marches, and a determination to use action to dramatize their message.

King and Lawson were powerless to stop the mayhem that followed in Memphis's Main Street as placards were turned into projectiles and hurled at police. Officers were soon forced to call for back-up when opportunistic bystanders joined demonstrators in the mass looting of downtown stores and the damaging of property. A distraught King was bundled away in a police car for his own safety, and driven to an out-of-town hotel away from the unrest. King was cut to the quick about the disorder, which had resulted in the police-related death of Larry Payne, numerous injuries, and property damage nearing half a million dollars. Mayor Loeb's officers took no prisoners in curtailing the disturbances – at one point corralling marchers into a church, where they tear-gassed them. The mayor matched this no-nonsense approach by bringing in the National Guard to enforce a dawn to dusk curfew.

King's increasing number of detractors waxed lyrical about his inability to maintain law and order, let alone non-violence, at his marches. The media, no doubt briefed by J. Edgar Hoover and politicos in Washington, warned that similar disorder would ensue if the PPC ever reached the

capital. In the aftermath of the Memphis disturbances, a forlorn King took to his bed where, fully clothed, he worried about the effects of the unrest on the Memphis campaign and his standing. Ralph Abernathy would later comment that he had never seen King so dejected, and even a late-night conversation with Coretta gave him no peace of mind. Never one who got a regular night's sleep, by 1968 King was suffering from chronic insomnia, sleeping for at most a couple of hours. Even foreign holidays provided no respite; earlier that year he took a short break with Abernathy to Mexico's Acapulco where, according to his friend, he spent the whole time worrying about the PPC and the SCLC. Abernathy, like others, was anxious about his friend's mental well-being, particularly his obsessive fatalism. King appeared willing to share his impending end with anyone who cared to listen, even treating his Ebenezer congregation to doses of doom in "The Drum Major Instinct" sermon, one of the last he was to deliver at his home church. Moreover, around this time he bought Coretta a bunch of plastic flowers, which he told her "would last, and be something by which she could remember him". His floral gift also doubled as a guilt offering for his constant absences, general inconsideration, and infidelities. (He had earlier broached the subject of his sexual peccadilloes with Coretta during her recuperation from painful hysterectomy surgery in January 1968.) Once again, it seemed that he wanted to set the record straight with God and humanity before meeting what he considered his impending denouement.

King left Memphis and returned to Atlanta. He continued to brood incessantly over the Memphis debacle and confessed to Abernathy that "Folks would now say Martin Luther King is finished." Yet such was his desire to finish off what he started he agreed to stage a further protest in

By 1968 President Lyndon
B. Johnson had become a
hate figure for those who
opposed his intervention in
Vietnam.

*If King was
unpopular with
his countrymen
over Vietnam, his
problems were small
compared to those of
President Johnson.*

Memphis on 5 April. Moreover, he had arranged to meet with members of
the Invaders, who were blamed by many for the Memphis disorder. Unlike
some of his more conservative peers, King's seemingly unshakeable belief
in his ideas meant he was always prepared to meet militants to discuss
everything from Black Power to non-violent direct action. The intellectual
in King found the exchange of ideas both challenging and stimulating. He
was against exclusion or sidelining, which he believed resulted in the types
of response seen in Memphis.

SCLC concerns about King's growing involvement in Memphis came
to a head at a meeting in Atlanta on 30 March, where he rounded on his
colleagues for their lack of support. Showing the kind of passion usually
reserved for his speeches, he attacked those who were using him to promote
their own agendas. Jesse Jackson faced the brunt of King's fury and after
one rather bruising exchange with his protégé, an angry King fled the room
with Jackson's pleas for him to return ringing in his ears. Once he had gone,
calm descended upon the meeting. After further discussions, SCLC staff
eventually acceded to King's demands and agreed to throw their efforts
behind the Memphis campaign. Word reached King of this resolution and
he returned to the scene of his earlier discomfiture, where a reconciliation
took place. He later dispatched Bevel, Williams, Jackson, and James E.
Orange to Memphis as an advance cadre to liaise with COME as well as the
Invaders to secure their non-violent involvement in the demonstration.

If King was unpopular with his countrymen over Vietnam, his problems
were small compared to those of President Johnson. Like King, LBJ's poll
ratings had been heading southward in direct proportion to the escalation
of the war in Vietnam and mounting US troop deaths. His standing reached

its nadir when the Viet Cong launched its audacious Tet Offensive campaign on 31 January 1968, which totally dispelled US and South Vietnamese pretensions of neutralizing the communist threat in the country. By March 1968, far too many Americans doubted the sanguine State Department press briefings about troop offensives in Vietnam. This scepticism became heightened the following month when over 500 US troops died in one week, resulting in the departure of the secretary of defense, Robert S. McNamara, and the inevitable calls for an increase in troop numbers to thwart the growing communist threat. A now sceptical US media compounded Johnson's problems by adopting the anti-Vietnam reportage style associated with countercultural publications such as *Ramparts*. LBJ, whose tenure in the White House had begun with the ambitious Great Society, was now a byword for warmongering and the subject of the chant "Hey, hey, LBJ, how many kids did you kill today?".

Like King, LBJ was a thoroughly depressed man by the early spring of 1968. He had spent the first few months of the year furiously discussing

I MAY NOT GET THERE WITH YOU

with aides the relative merits of running for a second term as president. His poor showing in the New Hampshire primaries against stalking-horse senator, Minnesota's Eugene McCarthy, and the decision of long-time adversary Robert Kennedy to run for president proved the deciding factors. With his grip on his party loosening and the Vietnam albatross hanging around his neck, a shell-shocked LBJ appeared on television on 31 March 1968 to tell the nation, "I shall not seek, and I will not accept, the nomination of my party for another term as your president." King received the news as he prepared for a Passion Sunday sermon at the capital's Washington Cathedral, where he once again returned to the themes that had so consumed him over the last year. He welcomed both LBJ's and Robert Kennedy's respective decisions as progressive for the USA, especially on the question of Vietnam and domestic poverty. According to one writer, King believed that a Kennedy victory in the 1968 presidential elections would "certainly result in a national rededication to the issues Martin was courageously expounding", and he even considered abandoning the PPC.

On 3 April a weary-looking King boarded a delayed flight from Atlanta Airport to Memphis. The bomb scare which had caused the delay only served to amplify his sense of foreboding. On arrival he checked into room 306 of the Lorraine, a motel run by African-American Lorraine Bailey, who counted King as a regular customer when he visited the city. His mood had lightened by the time he met with staff from COME to discuss the protest. His other meeting that day involved a strained conversation with the Invaders' Charles Cabbage, Calvin Taylor, and Charles Harrington, about their commitment to non-violence and proposed involvement in the march. The meetings, although useful, tired King and he resolved not to

"Because I've been to the mountaintop. And I don't mind. Like anybody, I would like to live a long time, longevity has its place. But I'm not concerned about that now. I just want to do God's will."

speak that evening at the huge Bishop Charles Mason Temple – the venue of his rapturously received speech on 18 March. Besides the unseasonably inclement weather plaguing Memphis, King decided to stay at the Lorraine to finish off a sermon he was going to call "Why America May Go to Hell", which he was due to deliver the next time he preached at Ebenezer. So as not to completely disappoint the crowd, he agreed to send Ralph Abernathy to the church to speak in his stead.

On his arrival at Mason Temple, Abernathy found a relatively small (for such a large church) but highly responsive congregation, and he placed a call to King at the Lorraine telling him to get down to the church quickly. King was persuaded and made the trip across town, taking his place in the pulpit, much to the delight of the highly excited throng. Alongside the "I Have a Dream" speech in Washington in 1963, his sermon that night, which proved his final one, was one of his most memorable. Like several of his speeches it was not original, and his SCLC colleagues seated in the church that night had heard it before. What they had not experienced was the intensity with which the sweat-covered King delivered it. He began by recounting his civil rights journey, his deep, booming voice emotionally recalling his near-fatal stabbing in 1958. Wiping the sweat from his brow he added: "Well, I don't know what will happen now. We've got some difficult days ahead, but it really doesn't matter to me now." Each phrase and sentence was punctuated by the accustomed congregational interjection of "Amen" or "Yes, sir"; the whirring of the fans inside the steaming church and the occasional thunderclap outside added atmosphere. King continued: "Because I've been to the mountaintop. And I don't mind. Like anybody, I would like to live a long time, longevity has its place. But I'm not concerned

> *"I may not get there with you. But I want you to know tonight that we, as a people, will get to the Promised Land. And so I'm happy tonight!"*

Below: "I may not get there with you": An emotional Martin Luther King delivers what would be his last speech on 3 April 1968.

Right: A simulated view through a gun sight of the balcony at the Lorraine Motel where Martin Luther King was shot and killed.

about that now. I just want to do God's will."

As a seasoned preacher and public speaker, King knew how to move a crowd, when to raise his voice or introduce a pregnant pause for greater effect, but that night his speech was without any stage-managed dramatics or showmanship. He was baring his soul to the largely black church crowd. This was very much the "Passion of King" played out in front of the media. And among the anguish and pain there was also power and strength, and it was a Spirit-filled King who delivered the lines, "And he's allowed me to go up to the mountain, and I've looked over, and I've seen the Promised Land!" The word "seen", which was drawn out into several syllables to express the gravity of the revelation, only increased the choruses of congregational affirmation and expectation. With tears welling in his eyes, King finished by saying: "I may not get there with you. But I want you to know tonight that we, as a people, will get to the Promised Land. And so I'm happy tonight! I'm not fearing any man! Mine eyes have seen the glory of the coming of the Lord!" With that he staggered back into his seat. His SCLC colleagues were as much enthused as they were disturbed by the passionate but chilling tone of his address. To the rapturous applause

of the congregation, King left the church and spent what would be his last earthly night in the company of a long-time female friend.

On the same day King arrived in Memphis, a white racist career criminal we now know as Nashville-born James Earl Ray checked into the less than salubrious Brewer's Rooming House, a stone's throw from the Lorraine Motel. Prior to his arrival, the forty-year-old fugitive from Missouri State Penitentiary had been travelling around the USA using various false names to evade arrest. Under his primary pseudonym, Eric S. (Starvo) Galt, he had appeared to be stalking King for nearly a month. Using the alias Harvey Lowmyer, Ray purchased a 760 Remington telescopic rifle, which he carried with him to Memphis a few days later when he booked into the rooming house under the name of John Willard. From his room's window, Ray could clearly see the Lorraine Motel with his newly purchased binoculars, but after rudimentary reconnaissance he realized there was a better view from the bathroom down the hallway.

On 4 April, a refreshed King awoke from his sleep around 10 a.m. and wasted no time in asking about Andrew Young and James Lawson's progress at the federal courthouse to obtain authorization for the protest. COME were having problems with City Hall, which was convinced that the proposed march would go the way of the previous one. With no news forthcoming, an anxious King opted for lunch at the Lorraine Motel's

café, where he shared a plate of catfish with Abernathy. He later chaired
a staff meeting to discuss the march, during which he stressed the
importance of it remaining non-violent, regardless of the provocation.
This led to a heated exchange with Hosea Williams, who had entered into
discussions about the SCLC hiring members of the Invaders "to teach
them non violence". King rebuffed Williams' idea, unconvinced of their
non-violent credentials. Just as he finished a further homily on the myriad
virtues of non-violence, Andrew Young returned with news that the
march could go ahead. Half in jest, King chided Young for his tardiness
and the two engaged in the mock pillow fights and physical joshing that
were a common occurrence in King's motels. Aware of the problems his
brother was facing, A. D. King had arrived from Louisville to offer some
support, and later that afternoon the brothers spoke at some length to
their mother in Atlanta.

3 April 1968: Martin Luther King on the balcony of the Lorraine Motel the day before he was shot. From left to right: Hosea Williams, Jesse Jackson, King and Ralph Abernathy.

Seconds later, a single shot from a rifle broke up the joviality and sent King crashing backwards to the balcony floor.

A more relaxed King then dressed for dinner at the Reverend Dr Samuel "Billy" Kyles' house. Dr Kyles was a Memphis colleague of James Lawson and an active member of COME. His wife, Gwen Kyles, was a splendid cook, and the Kyleses had promised to treat King and his friends to a sumptuous soul food banquet that night. But even the promise of a plateful of King's favourite food failed to hasten the tardy preacher, and at one point Dr Kyles gave him a friendly hurry-up to ensure he kept the dinner date and had time to attend a rally afterwards.

Around dusk, a fully dressed King stepped out onto the balcony to join his aides, who appeared demob happy. In the courtyard below, other SCLC staff and acquaintances were lingering, some of them play fighting, while the white Cadillac that was to take King to Dr Kyles' house was parked to one side, awaiting its famous passenger. Wanting to appear at his best, Abernathy ducked back into the motel room to splash on cologne, while King remained on the balcony discussing whether he should take his coat to stave off the evening chill. Seconds later, a single shot from a rifle broke up the joviality and sent King crashing backwards to the balcony floor – his bent legs protruding through the rails. Such was the bullet's velocity that it shattered his right jaw and cheek before severing his spinal cord. By the time Abernathy arrived to offer assistance, King was lying spreadeagled in a pool of blood. The silence rapidly turned to murmuring and then screaming, and the narrow balcony soon teemed with people, with one first-aider clumsily attempting to nurse King's wounds. Dr Kyles ran inside to call for an ambulance while Abernathy continued to forlornly encourage his colleague that it would be all right. When it became apparent that it would not be, he and Jesse Jackson drenched their hands and items of clothing respectively in their fallen hero's blood, as if they hoped this transferral would proffer some special blessing or power.

An ambulance took King to St Joseph's Hospital, where he was pronounced dead around an hour after being shot. The ever-faithful Abernathy was by his side in death as he was in life. It was also Abernathy who placed the call to Coretta to tell her the tragic news she had been expecting ever since her husband began his public work. (White extremist groups had been offering a bounty of tens of thousands of dollars on the head of "Martin Lucifer Coon". Moreover, the FBI had uncovered over fifty assassination plots to kill King; as a result, their agents had followed him to Memphis as much to spy on him as to supposedly protect him.)

If King's assassination hit America like an earthquake, the aftershocks reverberated around the world. Pope Paul VI spoke of his "profound sadness", the Danish prime minister saluted King's commitment to non-violence, while the (West) German parliament held a short, silent tribute. Sections of the Soviet press lambasted the US for the racism and violence that accounted for King, while one Ghanian publication argued that like all successful black leaders in the USA, he had been deliberately taken out. In the USA, his death evinced words of sympathy from the US president, who declared Sunday 7 April a day of mourning and made a decisive intervention in the Memphis sanitation strike. However, his appeals for calm went unheeded and King-related disturbances occurred in over 100 US cities, proving to be the most extensive inner city unrest the country had ever experienced. The disturbances in Washington came to within a few blocks of the White House, and were so fierce and sustained that a general on leave from Vietnam suggested the city resembled Saigon. In

"Soul Brother Number One", the singer James Brown, was credited with keeping the peace in Boston during the massive disturbances following Martin Luther King's assassination.

Chicago, the mercurial Mayor Daley called for a shoot to kill policy if the unrest encroached on the business district, while in Oakland, California, the police allegedly used the disturbances as a pretext to settle grievances against members of the Black Panthers. In Boston, the legendary African-American performer James Brown took part in a televised concert during which he appealed for calm and unity. Brown, who was known as "Soul Brother Number One" was credited with keeping the peace in that city in the days following King's murder. Elsewhere the deployment of around 100,000 soldiers and national guardsmen carried out the James Brown role, often meting out violence to quell the unrest. By the time most of the disturbances petered out, forty people, the majority African American, had lost their lives, and injuries were counted in their thousands.

After shooting King, James Earl Ray dumped his weapon on Memphis's South Main and made his getaway to Atlanta in a white Mustang car. The search for Ray became one of the largest manhunts in FBI history. Ray travelled to Canada, Britain, and Portugal on fake passports and was finally apprehended at Heathrow Airport in London on 8 June 1968 on his way to Brussels. He would eventually enter a guilty plea in exchange for not receiving the electric chair. As soon as he received his ninety-nine-year sentence, he recanted his plea and protested his innocence.

Martin Luther King's killing ranks alongside the assassination of JFK by Lee Harvey Oswald as grist to the mill for the conspiracy theorists. Debate raged over whether Ray was King's actual killer, and it was argued that he lacked the wherewithal to carry out such a well-planned operation. There was also speculation over whether he acted alone – it was suggested that King's killing could not have been the work of a lone gunman. Then there

Martin Luther King's funeral procession proceeds down West Hunter Street in Atlanta, Georgia, in April 1968.

were questions over Ray's motives; the convicted killer himself mentioned a mysterious figure named "Raoul", who was connected to some government plot. Moreover, because of King's anti-Vietnam and PPC activities it has been argued that Hoover's FBI played a nefarious role in his demise. Others such as Morehouse's Dr Benjamin Mays were more allegorical in their accusations, arguing that the killer was a product of a society that had vilified King, and had meant to cause him harm.

The fires in many US cities were still smouldering when on 8 April Coretta Scott King and her family members joined tens of thousands of marchers to complete the demo her husband had planned in support of the sanitation workers. The march was very much in honour of King, who was due to be buried the following day. His funeral itself took place in Atlanta at a packed Ebenezer Church and was attended by JFK's widow, Jacqueline Kennedy, Vice-President Hubert Humphrey (who deputized for the president, who did not attend for security reasons) and, because it was an election year, presidential candidates Robert Kennedy and Richard Nixon.

A serene Coretta led the mourners, alongside her now fatherless children and King's shell-shocked parents. As King had spoken so often of his demise it was agreed to use his "Drum Major" sermon as the eulogy. After the service two mules pulled his casket, which was borne on a wagon cart, through Atlanta's streets to Morehouse College, where Dr Benjamin Mays spoke, and King's favourite hymn "Precious Lord" was sung. King's casket was then taken to South View Cemetery where he was buried. His marble monument bore the poignant words, "Free at last, free at last, thank God Almighty, I'm free at last."

In keeping with King's wishes, Ralph Abernathy assumed the leadership of the SCLC and committed himself to continuing the work begun by his predecessor. One such legacy was the PPC, which was launched on 2 May 1968. One of the few positives of King's untimely demise was an upsurge in SCLC donations allowing the PPC to have a war chest of over a million dollars. The campaign began in earnest on 11 May with a rally at Cardozo High School Stadium in Washington. Unfortunately, the situation deteriorated after the buses, caravans, and an assortment of vehicles arrived in the capital to stay in "Resurrection City", an encampment near the Washington Monument. The camp became a byword for lawlessness and anti-social behaviour, attracting the attention of the forces of the law. What was meant to be one of the high points of the time in Washington, Solidarity Day, proved a damp squib that led to the resignation of Bayard Rustin, who had been drafted in to provide much-needed direction. A combination of mismanagement, press, public and political apathy, and poor weather contributed to the swift demise of Resurrection City. By mid June the encampment was seriously depleted, with only rabble-rousers left. On 24 June, a day after the site's permit expired, police moved in and began demolishing the "city". According to one writer, the SCLC was left with a $71,000 clean-up bill for Resurrection City.

Chapter 9
DREAMS TO REMEMBER

It would be an understatement to suggest that the Reverend Dr Martin Luther King Jr was a hard act to follow, and his designated successor Ralph Abernathy struggled to hold together a movement that was already fragmenting. With the one cohesive force gone, the key SCLC figures went their own way, mostly opting for roles in public life. Andrew Young moved into politics, winning a seat as a Democratic congressman for Georgia in the early 1970s. In 1977, the Democratic president Jimmy Carter appointed him as Ambassador to the United Nations, and in 1980 he was elected as mayor of Atlanta. Another stalwart, Jesse Jackson, also segued into mainstream politics. After building up the Operation Breadbasket programme in Chicago, he established People United to Save Humanity to replicate its predecessor's work nationally. Jackson launched bold bids for the White House in 1984 and 1988 as the head of the Rainbow Coalition, a multi-ethnic entity echoing King's "I Have a Dream" paradigm.

Politics were much in evidence in the campaign to have a Martin Luther King Jr Day national holiday in the USA. Once King had been laid to rest, a Democrat congressman introduced a bill to Congress to make King's birthday a public holiday. Although there had been much "artificially generated homage" to King after his death, there was little appetite for such a move in Washington, on the grounds of costs (a paid holiday for workers) and that King had never held public office. Nevertheless, the movement gained traction through the King Center's campaign, and the involvement of African-American singer/songwriter Stevie Wonder, whose international smash hit "Happy Birthday" (1980) was a paean calling on the US to officially mark what was King's birthday. This was followed by a colossal petition calling on

The 40th Anniversary of the "I Have A Dream" Speech

Celebrating

Congress to pass the law. On 2 November 1983, US president Ronald Reagan signed into law a bill creating a federal holiday in honour of King. (Ironically, Reagan had been an opponent of King while governor of California in the 1960s.) The third Monday in January, which falls closest to King's birthday on 15 January, is now observed as a national holiday in the USA.

The widowed Coretta Scott King picked up her late husband's torch and continued aspects of his civil rights efforts, as well as developing her own work on gender and human sexuality. Aside from raising her four growing children, she was instrumental in establishing the monumental legacy foundation, the King Center in Atlanta, Georgia. A part of this project involved the initiation of the King Papers Project, which began in 1985 under the direction of Stanford University academic Clayborne Carson. Dr Carson was tasked to "publish a definitive fourteen-volume edition of King's most significant correspondence, sermons, speeches, published writings, and unpublished manuscripts" and to use multimedia

African Americans in Washington mark the 40th anniversary of the March on Washington and Martin Luther King's iconic "I Have a Dream" speech in 2003.

Coretta Scott King picked up her late husband's torch and continued aspects of his civil rights efforts, as well as developing her own work on gender and human sexuality.

and information technology to promote King's ideas and achievements. Moreover, Coretta carefully tended her husband's image to ensure it remained in the popular psyche, and tenaciously oversaw the running of the King Estate, which involved maintaining control over the lucrative intellectual property issues linked to the civil rights leader.

This last aspect has drawn criticism over the way King's image has been used since his death. Disapproval has also been levelled at the public spat between the King Center and Boston University over his papers. Other controversies involved the eleventh-hour financial intervention of business and civic leaders to buy King's personal papers which were due to be auctioned off at Sotheby's in New York.

Despite the fact that King has been dead longer than he lived, there appears to be no diminution of interest in him. As well as books, there has been a recent slew of plays, documentaries, and films, all examining aspects of his life. Moreover, any examination of civil rights, the 1960s, or US history invariably includes a feature on him.

The Reverend Dr Martin Luther King Jr was one of the seminal figures of the twentieth century. His worth to the United States has been inestimable; he was one of the few people who could be the conscience of a nation that has always prided itself on liberty, but for so long denied too many of its people this much-vaunted freedom. Martin Luther King went some way toward redeeming this inherent contradiction. Yet he has transcended the USA and belongs to the world.

Since time immemorial, scholars have pondered over what is the "measure of a man". Indeed, King even used the phrase as the title of one of his early published works. What is the "measure of King"; that is, how

should he be assessed in our modern, ultra-critical world? There is little doubt that he was a great man who changed the history of the USA and whose influence has been felt in various parts of the world. Yet he was also a flawed individual who at times failed to practise what he preached. He clearly did not live out the Christian imperative of monogamy, and his views on women, especially toward his wife, now appear chauvinistic. Although he was a charismatic leader, his actual leadership of the SCLC often lacked the ability to make authoritative and potentially divisive decisions. Additionally, he was at times too cautious when addressing those in power, and arguably too trusting of those he believed could be changed.

These idiosyncrasies undoubtedly reveal that, like most, he was a complex combination of saint and sinner; a human being with common strengths and weaknesses. What is more, he was very much cognizant of these flaws and alluded to them sporadically in his sermons. As a result, he would never have wanted the hagiographies and sanctification that he has been afforded since his death. After all, this was a man who in a section of his famed "The Drum Major Instinct" speech argued that his Nobel Peace Prize was not important, nor were his "three or four hundred other awards". For all the accolades heaped upon him, he remained a humble man who

Left: The crypt which houses the body of Martin Luther King at the King Center in Atlanta, Georgia.

Right: US Senate candidate Barack Obama speaks at the Democratic National Convention in Boston, Massachusetts, on 27 July 2004.

refused to be seduced by the twin totems of money and power. Unlike the many financial scandals affecting far too many politicians and preachers today, he lived frugally. In fact, he longed for a Gandhi-style existence where he could divest himself of all material goods. What mattered to him was that he did the right thing on a range of crucial ethical and political issues of the day.

Had he lived, he would probably have opposed the US-led interventions in Iraq and Afghanistan, and he would also have been critical of the unfettered capitalism that led to the financial crisis of 2008. Although he would probably have endorsed the election of the first black US president, Barak Obama, King circa 1968 would have remained a critical friend of the black commander-in-chief's foreign policy. All this remains conjecture since King is dead, and it can be argued that his latter-day radicalism would have put him in the firing line of other would-be assassins.

It would be wrong to suggest that the civil rights movement would not have taken place had there been no Martin Luther King – a movement is invariably bigger than one human being, and history shows that the struggle for African-American rights clearly predated him. Moreover, African Americans have had no shortage of "leaders" throughout their history in the USA. Having said that, King was an extraordinary leader, with the ability to galvanize the support and commitment of those with an interest in black rights. He also had the amazing capacity to inspire and embolden those who, for a number of reasons, had failed to engage in the struggle. Equally as important was his calm, measured approach, which tended to put most white people at ease, and an inclusiveness that clearly encouraged liberals to be part of his movement for change. His conservative radicalism

A photograph of the Reverend
Dr Martin Luther King Jr in 1967.

meant that he was equally disposed to meet politicians in the White House and militants in the community centre. As well as being media savvy, in terms of his own image, he also leveraged these news-focused outlets to great effect during his campaigns.

Even the various exposés of the apparent seamier side of his life have not tarnished his image or relevance. If anything, they have stripped away the myth behind the man and enabled aficionados to discover the real Martin Luther King Jr. Far from being a dreamer who needed to wake up, his vision continues to inspire. His message still remains the standard-bearer for hope in a world often bereft of such expectation, and his belief in personal and social transformation still speaks to individuals and communities desperate for real and lasting change.

ENDNOTES

Chapter 1

1. Richard Wayne Wills Sr, *Martin Luther King and the Image of God*, Oxford: Oxford University Press, 2009, p. 33.

2. John White, *Black Leadership in America: Booker T. Washington to Jesse Jackson*, Second edition, London and New York: Longman, 1990, p. 5.

3. Anthony B. Pinn, *Terror and Triumph: The Nature of Black Religion*, Minneapolis, MN: Augsburg Fortress, 2003, p. 90.

4. John White, *op. cit.*

5. Anthony B. Pinn, *op. cit.*

6. Eric Foner, *The Story of American Freedom*, W. W. Norton & CO, 1999, p. 89.

7. Nathan Hare, *Black Anglo-Saxons*, Second edition, Chicago, IL: Third World Press, 2006, p. 1.

8. John White, *op. cit.*

9. Ronald Segal, *The Race War: The Worldwide Conflict of Races*, London: Penguin Books, 1966, pp. 230–31.

10. Colin Grant, *Negro with a Hat: The Rise and Fall of Marcus Garvey and His Dream of Mother Africa*, London: Jonathan Cape, 2008, p. 302.

Chapter 2

1. Taylor Branch, *Parting the Waters: America in the King Years, 1954-63*, London: Simon and Schuster, 1988, p. 59.

2. Stephen B. Oates, *Let the Trumpet Sound: A Life of Martin Luther King, Jr*, New York: Harper Perennial, 1994, p. 41.

3. Richard Wayne Wills Sr, *op. cit.*

4. David L. Lewis, *King: A Biography*, Second edition, IL: University of Illinois Press, 1978, p. 28.

5. Martin Luther King Jr, *Stride Toward Freedom*, New York: Harper & Row, 1958.

6. Roger Bruns, *Martin Luther King Jr: A Biography*, CT: Greenwood Press, 2006, p. 18.

7. Taylor Branch, *op. cit.*

8. Roger Bruns, *op. cit.*

9. Warren E. Steinkraus, "Martin Luther King's personalism and non-violence", *Journal of the History of Ideas*, Vol. 34, No. 1, January–March 1973, PA: University of Pennsylvania Press, pp. 97 –111.

10. Richard Lischer, *The Preacher King: Martin Luther King Jr, and the Word That Moved America*, Oxford: Oxford University Press, 1997, pp. 108–13

11. Michael Eric Dyson, *I May Not Get There with You: The True Martin Luther King Jr*, New York: Touchstone, 2001, pp. 139–54.

12. Richard Lischer, *op. cit.*

13. It took the assassination of M. L. for Coretta Scott King to realize something of her true leadership capabilities.

Chapter 3

1. David L. Lewis, *op. cit.*

2. Taylor Branch, *op. cit.*

3. David L. Lewis, *King: A Biography*, Illini Books, 1978, p. 63.

4. Philip Jenkins, *A History of the United States*, Third edition, Basingstoke: Palgrave Macmillan, 2007, p. 262.

5. Often this meant black passengers paying at the front, getting off, and reboarding at the back door.

6. Jo Ann Robinson and David J Garrow, *Montgomery Bus Boycott and the Women Who Started it: The Memoir of Jo Ann Gibson Robinson*, TN: University of Tennessee Press, pp. 43–49.

7. John White, *op. cit.*

8. Rosa Parks and James Haskins, *Rosa Parks: My Story*, New York: Dial Books, 1992, p. 136.

9. Michael Eric Dyson, *op. cit.*

Chapter 4

1. Clayborne Carson ed., *Autobiography of Martin Luther King Jr*, London: Abacus, 2000, p. 99.

2. Dennis C. Dickerson, *Militant Mediator, Whitney M. Young Jr*, KY: University Press of Kentucky, 2004, p. 5.

3. An apocryphal story surrounds Nixon's visit to the independence celebrations in Ghana in 1957. It is said that the then US vice-president kept greeting every black person he met with the question, 'How does it feel to be free?' On one occasion he greeted a black man at a function with this question. The man shook his head and replied, "I wouldn't know anything about being free. I'm from Mississippi!"

4. Louis Fischer, *The Life of Mahatma Gandhi*, London: HarperCollins, 1997, pp. 102–3.

5. Fred Powledge, *Free at Last? The Civil Rights Movement and the People Who Made it*, London: Little, Brown and Company, 1991, p. 211.

6. David Reynolds, *America, Empire of Liberty: A New History*, London: Penguin Books, 2010, p. 416.

7. Alan Farmer and Vivienne Sanders, *An Introduction to American History 1860–1990*, Hodder & Stoughton, 2002, p. 289.

8. Nick Bryant *The Bystander: John F. Kennedy and the Struggle for Black Equality*, New York: Basic Books, 2006, p. 166.

9. Robert Dallek, *John F. Kennedy: An Unfinished Life*, London: Penguin Books, 2003, p. 215.

10. Robert Dallek, *op cit.*

11. Nick Bryant, *op cit.*

12. Thomas C. Reeves, *A Question of Character: A Life of John F. Kennedy*, New York: Arrow Books, 1991, p. 340.

13. Godfrey Hodgson, *Martin Luther King*, London: Quercus, 2009, p. 79.

Chapter 5

1. David J. Garrow, *Bearing the Cross: Martin Luther King and the Southern Christian Leadership Conference*, London: Jonathan Cape, 1986, p. 312.

2. See Diane McWhorter, *Carry Me Home: Birmingham, Alabama: The Climatic Battle of the Civil Rights Revolution*, London: Simon & Schuster, 2002.

3. Glenn T. Eskew. *But for Birmingham: The Local and National Movements in the Civil Rights Struggle*, NC: The University of North Carolina Press, 1997, pp. 261–63.

4. By 1963 King was regarded as someone who could steer the USA away from the brink of racial violence and chaos.

5. Michael Eric Dyson, *op. cit.*

6. Robert Dallek, *op. cit.*

Chapter 6

1. Michael Eric Dyson, *Making Malcolm: The Myth and Meaning of Malcolm X*, Oxford: Oxford University Press, 1995, p. 90.

2. Michael Eric Dyson, *I Might Not Get There with You: The True Martin Luther King Jr*, New York: Touchstone, 2001, p. 160.

3. Stewart Burns, *To the Mountaintop: Martin Luther King Jr's Sacred Mission to Save America: 1955–1968*, New York: HarperCollins, 2004, p. 490.

4. John A. Kirk, *Martin Luther King Jr*, New York: Longman, 2004, pp. 120–21.

5. David J. Garrow, *Protest at Selma: Martin Luther King Jr, and the Voting Rights Acts of 1965*, New Haven: Yale University Press, 1978, p. 61.

Chapter 7

1. Joyce A. Ladner, "White America's Response to Black Militancy in Black Americans", ed. John F. Szwed, *Voice of America Forum Lectures*, 1970, p. 224.

2. Godfrey Hodgson, *op. cit.*

3. Kevern Verney, *Black Civil Rights in America*, London and New York: Routledge, 2000, p. 61.

4. Stokely Carmichael and Charles V. Hamilton, *Black Power: The Politics of Liberation in America*, London: Penguin Books, 1967, p. 67.

5. Martin Luther King Jr, *Where Do We Go from Here: Chaos or Community?*, New York: Harper & Row, 1967.

6. Adam Fairclough, "Was Martin Luther King a Marxist?", ed. John A. Kirk, *Martin Luther King, Jr and the civil rights movement: Controversies and debates*, Palgrave Macmillan, 2007, p. 187.

7. Taylor Branch, *At Canaan's Edge: America in the King Years, 1965-68*, London: Simon & Schuster, 2006, p. 443.

8. Daniel Patrick Moynihan, "The Negro Family: The Case For National Action", Office of Policy Planning and Research, United States Department of Labor, March 1965.

9. Robert Dallek, *Lyndon B. Johnson: Portrait of a President*, London: Penguin, 2005, p. 280.

Chapter 8

1. Marshall Frady, *Martin Luther King, Jr: A Life*, London: Penguin Books, 2002, pp. 196–7.

2. Stewart Burns, *op. cit.*, p. 402.

3. R. Jeffreys-Jones, *The FBI: A History*, Yale University Press, 2007, pp. 170–71.

BIBLIOGRAPHY

Abernathy, Ralph, *And the Walls Came Tumbling Down*, New York: Harper & Row, 1989.

Branch, Taylor, *Parting the Waters: America in the King Years 1954–63*, London: Simon and Schuster, 1988.

Branch, Taylor, *Pillar of Fire: America in the King Years, 1963–65*, New York: Touchstone, 1999.

Branch, Taylor, *At Canaan's Edge: America in the King Years, 1965–68*, London: Simon & Schuster, 2006.

Bruns, Roger, *Martin Luther King, Jr: A Biography*, CT: Greenwood Press, 2006.

Bryant, Nick, *The Bystander: John F. Kennedy and the Struggle for Black Equality*, New York: Basic Books, 2006.

Burns, Stewart, *To the Mountaintop: Martin Luther King Jr's Sacred Mission to Save America: 1955–1968*, New York: HarperCollins, 2004.

Carmichael, Stokely, and Hamilton, Charles V., *Black Power: The Politics of Liberation in America*, London: Penguin Books, 1967.

Carson, Clayborne et al, *The Eyes on the Prize – Civil Rights Reader. Documents, speeches, and firsthand accounts from the black freedom struggle, 1954–1990*, London: Penguin Books, 1991.

Cone, James H., *Martin & Malcolm & America: A Dream or a Nightmare?* New York: Orbis Books, 1992.

Crawford, Vicki L., Rouse, Jacqueline Anne, Woods, Barbara (eds.), *Women in the Civil Rights Movement: Trailblazers and Torchbearers, 1941–1965*, IN: Indiana University Press, 1993.

Dallek, Robert, *John F. Kennedy: An Unfinished Life*, London: Penguin Books, 2003

Dallek, Robert, *Lyndon B. Johnson: Portrait of a President*, London: Penguin Books, 2005.

Davis, Jack E. (ed.), *The Civil Rights Movement*, Malden: Blackwell Publishers, 2001.

Dyson, Michael Eric, *I May Not Get There with You: The True Martin Luther King Jr*, New York: Touchstone, 2001.

Fairclough, Adam, *Martin Luther King Jr*, GA: University of Georgia Press, 1995.

Fischer, Louis, *The Life of Mahatma Gandhi*, London: HarperCollins, 1997.

Frady, Marshall, *Martin Luther King, Jr: A Life*, London: Penguin Books, 2002.

Garrow, David J., *Bearing the Cross: Martin Luther King, Jr and the Southern Christian Leadership Conference*, London: Jonathan Cape, 1988.

Harding, Vincent, *Martin Luther King: The Inconvenient Hero*, New York: Orbis Books, 2008.

Hodgson, Godfrey, *Martin Luther King*, London: Quercus, 2009.

King, Coretta Scott, *My Life with Martin Luther King, Jr*, New York: Holt, Rinehart & Winston, 1969.

King, Martin Luther Jr, *Strength to Love*, London: Fount, 1980.

King, Martin Luther Jr, *Letter from Birmingham Jail/I Have a Dream Speech* (Tale Blazer), IA: Perfection Learning, 1990.

King, Martin Luther Sr, *Daddy King: An Autobiography*, New York: William Morrow & Co, 1980.

Kirk, John A., *Martin Luther King, Jr*, New York: Longman, 2004.

King, Martin Luther Jr, Carson, Clayborne (ed.), *Autobiography of Martin Luther King, Jr*, London: Abacus, 2000.

Kirk, John A. (ed.), *Martin Luther King, Jr and the Civil Rights Movement: Controversies and debates*, Basingstoke: Palgrave Macmillan, 2007.

Lewis, David L., *King: A Biography*, Second edition, IL: University of Illinois Press, 1978.

Ling, Peter J., *Martin Luther King, Jr*, London and New York: Routledge, 2002.

Lischer, Richard, *The Preacher King: Martin Luther King, Jr and the Word that Moved America*, Oxford: Oxford University Press, 1997.

Lomax, Louis E., *To Kill a Black Man*, Los Angeles: Holloway House, 1987.

Malcolm X, *The Autobiography of Malcolm X*, London: Penguin Books, 1965.

Reynolds, David, *America, Empire of Liberty: A New History*, London: Penguin Books, 2010.

Riches, William T., *The Civil Rights Movement: Struggle and Resistance*, Second edition, Basingstoke: Palgrave Macmillan, 2004.

Sitkoff, Harvard, *King: Pilgrimage to the Mountaintop*, New York: Hill and Wang, 2007.

Washington, Booker T., *Up From Slavery*, Oxford: Oxford World's Classics, 2008.

White, John, *Black Leadership in America: Booker T. Washington to Jesse Jackson*, Second edition, New York: Longman, 1990.

Journals

"Stepping back into the frame. Freedom riders of 1961", *American Legacy*, 14/3, Fall 2008.

Magazines

Simeon Booker, "50,000 March on Mississippi: Martin Luther King leads Negroes, whites in most heroic civil rights protest in history", *Ebony*, Vol. 19, No. 11, September 1964.

Websites

Stanford University: King Papers Project: http://mlk-kpp01.stanford.edu/index.php/kingpapers/article/what_is_the_king_papers_project/

INDEX

A

Abernathy, Reverend Ralph David 42, 44, 55, 65–66, 73, 88–89, 119, 122, 131, 139, 162, 163, 167, 170–72, 176–77

Albany Movement 86–90

Ali, Muhammad 153–54

Atlanta, Georgia 10–11, 15, 16, 19, 24, 26–27, 40, 60, 64, 66, 71–73, 76, 81, 88, 124, 128, 143, 163–64, 173–74, 177–78

B

Baker, Ella 61, 64–65, 72, 76, 77

Belafonte, Harry 35, 100, 108, 135

Beloved Community 34, 148, 158–59

Bevel, James 73, 96, 100–102, 134, 139–40, 143, 158, 164

Birmingham, Alabama 82, 90, 98, 110–13, 122, 148

Birmingham campaign 93–104, 107, 118, 138

Black Power 116, 147–50, 152, 164

Black Panthers 150, 173

"Bombingham" 95

Bombings 59, 94–95, 103, 110–12, 151–52

Boston University 33–35, 42, 179

Brown v. Board of Education (1954) 47, 53

C

Carmichael, Stokely 116–18, 146–47

Chicago campaign 143–50

Civil Rights Act (1964) 114

Clark, Sheriff James (Jim) 132–34

Communism 30–31, 61, 107, 112, 121, 131, 152, 156, 159, 165

Congress of Racial Equality (CORE) 60, 82, 106, 124, 146, 159

Connor, Theophilus Eugene (Bull) 96–97, 100–103, 132

Cotton, Dorothy 77, 121, 131, 155

Crozer Theological Seminary 27, 29–34

Crusade for Citizenship 62, 64

D

Daley, Mayor Richard J. 144, 149, 173

Dexter Avenue Baptist Church 41–45, 71

Deep South, The 30, 82–83, 139–43, 158

E

Ebenezer Baptist Church (Atlanta) 16–18, 23, 29, 31, 40–42, 72, 143, 154, 163, 167, 174

F

Farmer, James (CORE) 60, 82–83

Federal Bureau of Investigation (FBI) 92–93, 112, 119–20, 126, 129, 159, 172–74

Fellowship for Reconciliation (FOR) 58

Forman, James (SNCC and Black Panthers) 73, 118, 119

Freedom Rides 82, 84

G

Gandhi, Mohandas Karamchand (Mahatma) 31, 33, 57–58, 60, 67–70, 84, 89, 158, 181

Garvey, Marcus Mosiah 23

Ghana 8, 65, 78, 81

H

Hamer, Fannie Lou 126–27

Hoover, J. Edgar 92–93, 112, 119–20, 129, 159, 162, 174

I

"I Have a Dream" 108–111, 167, 178

India 31, 60, 67–70

Invaders 162, 164, 166, 170

J

Jackson, Jesse L. 149–50, 158, 164, 170–72, 177

Jackson, Jimmie Lee 132, 135, 137
Johnson, Lyndon B. 113–15, 127, 129, 135, 137, 151–52, 164–65
Johnson, Mordecai 31, 69

K

Kennedy, John F. 66, 78–82, 91–92, 104–112, 114, 115
Kennedy, Robert F. 83–84, 92, 155–56, 166, 174
King, Martin Luther Sr (Daddy) 15–19, 23–26, 29–30, 33, 37–42, 56, 60, 71–72, 82, 139
King, Martin Luther Jr 41, 50, 85, 101, 125, 144, 152, 168, 182
  Assassination 171–72
  Birth 15
  Childhood 18, 26–28
  Education 27–40, 42–44
  Extra-marital affairs 92, 119–20, 129, 163, 169
  Family 51, 67, 85–86, 96, 119
  Funeral 174–75
  Imprisonment 55–56, 81, 88–89, 100, 122, 132
  Marriage to Coretta Scott 35–40, 85–86, 119, 129, 163
  Nobel Peace Prize 128–30, 153, 180
  Politics 66, 78–82, 98–100, 104–115, 126–35, 151–66
  Speeches 51–52, 57, 62–64, 108–109, 122, 129–31, 136–37, 166–68
  Writings 66–67, 98, 128, 148
Ku Klux Klan 18, 21, 94–95, 103–104, 110, 121, 126, 135

L

Lawson, Revd James 69, 70, 146, 160–62, 169, 171
Letter from Birmingham Jail 98, 128

Levison, Stanley 61–62, 67, 71, 78, 112, 121
Lewis, John 73, 83, 108, 132, 134, 146
Lincoln, Abraham 20–21, 64, 78, 92, 109
Lorraine Motel (Memphis) 166–72

M

Malcolm X 35, 100, 105–107, 116, 132, 134, 146, 148
March on Washington (1963) 107–111, 178
March to Montgomery 134–35
Marx, Karl 30–31, 38, 156
McKissick, Floyd 146
Memphis, Tennessee 146, 160–73
Memphis Sanitation Workers campaign 160, 172, 174
Meredith, James 90–92, 145–46
Meredith march 146–48
Mississippi Freedom Summer 124–26
Morehouse College 17, 27–29, 33, 174
Moses, Bob 126

N

Nation of Islam 105, 146, 159 *see also* Malcolm X
National Association for the Advancement of Colored People (NAACP) 19, 23–24, 38, 45–49, 56–57, 60, 62, 65, 72–74, 78, 95, 106–107, 121, 124, 142, 150, 153, 158, 160
National Urban League 24, 60, 150, 153, 156
Nixon, E. D. 45–49, 51, 57
Nixon, Richard M. 65–66, 78, 82, 174
Nobel Peace Prize *see under* King, Martin Luther Jr
Non-violence 28, 57–61, 69–73, 86–92, 98, 102–104, 116–19, 132, 142, 146, 162–64, 170

O

Operation Breadbasket 149–50, 158, 177 *see also* Jackson, Jesse L.

P

Parks, Rosa 46–52
Poor People's Campaign 12, 157
Powell, Adam Clayton 24, 78, 118
Prayer Pilgrimage 61–63
Project "C" 93
Project Mississippi *see* Mississippi Freedom
 Summer

R

Randolph, A. Philip 24, 62, 78, 107
Ray, James Earl 169, 173–74
Resurrection City 176
Robinson, Jo Ann 46, 49
Rustin, Bayard 57–58, 61–62, 67, 69, 71, 78,
 107–108, 121, 131, 153, 158, 160, 176

S

St Augustine, Florida 101, 121–24, 126,
 128, 148
Scott, Coretta 36, 39, 42, 51, 56–57, 69–71,
 85–86, 112, 119, 128–32, 153, 163
 Childhood 38
 Education 38
 Maintaining King's legacy 174, 178–79
 Marriage *see under* King, Martin Luther Jr
Segregation 15, 17–26, 32, 37–38, 45–61,
 79, 86–92, 104, 120–22, 132, 139, 144
Selma campaign 133–39
Sit-ins 73–76, 82, 86, 87, 97, 121
Slavery 20–24, 30, 150
Southern Christian Leadership Conference
 (SCLC) 34, 60–77, 82–98, 103, 106–107,
 119–131, 137–45, 149–71, 176–77, 180
Student Nonviolent Coordinating Committee
 (SNCC) 72–73, 82–89, 106, 108, 116,
 119, 121, 124, 131–42, 145–47, 159

T

Till, Emmett 46–47, 104
Tillich, Paul 32, 34, 40
Time-Life magazine 82

V

Vietnam War 131, 151-56, 158, 164-66, 174

W

Walker, Wyatt Tee (SCLC) 76-77, 88, 93, 97,
 128, 139
Wallace, Governor George 104, 134, 135,
 139, 160
Washington, Booker T. 22-23, 27
"We Shall Overcome" 135, 137
Wilkins, Roy (NAACP) 56-57, 60, 62, 64-65,
 76, 79, 107-108, 114
Williams, Hosea 121, 134, 139, 164, 170

Y

Young, Andrew 77, 139, 158, 160, 169-70,
 177
Young, Whitney 108, 114, 154-56

Alamy ... nd Arts
Photo ... Minds;
p. 145 ...

Corbis ... 9, 123,
125, 1 ... in Van
Hasselt ... tz/dpa;
p. 21 H ... 6 Steve
Schapir ... ary of
Congre ... p. 175
James L

Getty: ... 47, 49,
50, 56, ... Y Daily
News; ...

iStock:

Topfot